The Secret Country

An interpretation of the folklore
of ancient sites in the British Isles

An interpretation of the folklore of ancient sites in the British Isles

The
Secret
Country

Janet and Colin Bord

 WALKER AND COMPANY · NEW YORK

By the same authors
Mysterious Britain

By Janet Bord
Ghosts
Mazes and Labyrinths of the World

ISBN: 0-8027-0559-6

Library of Congress Catalog Card Number: 76-50419

Printed in the United States of America

10   9   8   7   6   5   4   3   2   1

Contents

Acknowledgements

Most of the illustrations come from our own collection, but we are grateful to the following for permission to reproduce material which is their copyright: Trustees of the British Museum (on pages 28 (bottom) and 179); Hamish Campbell (page 40); National Museum of Antiquities of Scotland (page 63:4); The Pitt Rivers Museum, Oxford (page 63:3); Geoffrey N. Wright (page 112).

We also thank the following publishers for giving us permission to reproduce copyright material: B. T. Batsford Ltd, for extracts from *Welsh Country Upbringing* by D. Parry-Jones; Blackie and Son Ltd, for an extract from *Scottish Folk-Lore and Folk Life* by Donald A. Mackenzie; Pitman Publishing Ltd and Abelard-Schuman Publishing Co., for extracts from *The Pattern of the Past* by Guy Underwood; Routledge & Kegan Paul Ltd, for extracts from *The Legend of the Sons of God, ESP Beyond Time and Distance, Witches,* and *Ghost and Ghoul* by T. C. Lethbridge; Shire Publications Ltd, for extracts from *The Early Barrow-Diggers* by Barry M. Marsden; and Colin Smythe Ltd, for extracts from *The Middle Kingdom* by D. A. Mac Manus.

To the Reader

We hope not only that you will enjoy this book, but also that it will make you think about the *unwritten* history of the British Isles. Some of the ideas we have outlined may seem incredible at first, and it is true that there is an apparently uncrossable gulf between the theories we present and the beliefs held by most people. But an exploratory bridge is being built across the gulf, as more and more people are taking an interest in seemingly inexplicable phenomena, and those who have kept abreast of developments in the fields of parapsychology and the 'fringe' sciences will realise that the subject-matter of this book cannot be so easily dismissed. However, until more practical research is undertaken, the majority of our ideas must remain theoretical, and we have tried to make this clear throughout the book, by qualifying our statements where necessary. Traditions have on occasion not been qualified, because it is clear that they are usually symbolic; and any apparently definite statements we make when dealing with ideas rather than facts should be understood as being our personal beliefs.

All historical research into unrecorded events must of necessity remain speculative, especially the further away one gets from the present. Therefore, every reader is free to accept or reject anything he or she reads in these pages.

Janet and Colin Bord
Powys, January 1976

I Earth currents in tradition and theory

'the mysterious earth-currents which thrill the clay of our bodies'
Rudyard Kipling, *Kim*

Britain's ancient past, the time before the arrival of the Romans, is shrouded in mystery. The general picture held by most people is of a land of savages, living degraded lives in caves or rough huts, meeting together every so often to erect a Stonehenge or Silbury Hill at the dictates of the priests. Then the Romans came and civilised them, and the march of progress has continued ever since. It is tacitly assumed that our distant ancestors were ignorant and dull-witted, and that our present attitudes and mode of life must be superior in every way. Undoubtedly there are some people who do not hold these views. Today especially there is a wide interest in prehistory, from both the archaeological and mystical approaches. Archaeologists sieve the soil for the material fragments that remain from earlier civilisations; while mediums tune in to other-dimensional sources of knowledge. Both approaches produce results, and any individual's acceptance of them must depend on his own inclination. However, it is not the intention of this book to investigate either of these avenues, for our research into the nature of the people of prehistoric Britain follows another line, that of folklore.

During the period between the end of the last Ice Age and the arrival of the Romans, a period of approximately 4,000 years, a great number of structures were raised throughout the British Isles. Still remaining are 1,500–2,000 megalithic tombs, 10,000–20,000 round barrows, 200 long barrows, many hundreds of stone circles, several thousand hillforts, and countless thousands of standing stones, with lesser numbers of henges, settlements, and cursuses. How many more have been destroyed by the encroachments of man during the past 2,000 years? There are traditions connected with many ancient sites which might, if carefully interpreted, provide new insights into the nature, abilities, and beliefs of prehistoric man. There are risks, of course, in following such a line of research, one being that we rarely have any means of knowing how old any particular tradition is. But even if a tradition is relatively recent, perhaps only 500 years old, it still indicates the attitude of the originator towards the ancient site to which it relates, and this attitude would itself be based on inherited attitudes.

One feature of many of the traditions we shall include in the following chapters is their apparent absurdity. A good example (from Chapter Six, where an interpretation is attempted) is the story of the Bonnet Stone in Kinveachy Woods (Highland: formerly Inverness)* where a giant hid his heart; he moved it to another stone if he saw a man wearing a bonnet anywhere near the stone, because the only way to kill the heart was to lay a

Opposite: Long Meg, Cumbria

*The method of presentation of old and new county names is explained at the end of this chapter.

bonnet on the stone while the heart was still in it. It is easy to dismiss such tales as stemming from an illiterate and apparently stupid peasantry. But folk traditions are not conceived in a vacuum, and if carefully considered they can, we believe, often be found to have a factual basis. Their interpretation of course varies according to the interpreter; but it is surprising how many of the folk traditions of Britain's ancient sites fit in with the ideas we hold concerning the original usages the ancient sites were put to. The traditions are often superficially inane, but this is probably because the people who originated them did not understand the events and effects they were trying to describe. By the time the traditions began to be developed, the events they described must have remained in memory only, or been closely guarded by an elite or priesthood (though this may not have been the case originally), and the populace tried to explain the incomprehensible by inventing stories that today appear to us to be equally incomprehensible. A modern parallel can be seen in the cargo cults of Melanesia, which started around the 1880s in Fiji. One aspect of the cults in their modern form involves copying the outer appearances of Western civilisation—for example the natives make model aeroplanes and construct dummy airstrips, believing that they will attract planes loaded with cargo, such as those which brought Red Cross medical supplies during the war. They misunderstand the forces they are dealing with; and the traditions we recount in this book exhibit the same characteristic.

If there were few traditions relating to the ancient sites of the British Isles, it would be fruitless to try to deduce anything from them. However, there are many, and the 650 we include by no means exhaust the material. Although the data is in many ways imprecise, we nevertheless feel that the cumulative effect of the mass of tradition that has persisted through the centuries is such as to indicate that the ancient sites of the British Isles had significances and functions which are far removed from the interpretations we are familiar with today.

A growing interest in Britain's past has resulted in the development of a number of unconventional, non-academic theories. Some of these are relevant to our study, so our intention is to draw a number of such threads together, and see how they relate to the folklore of the ancient sites. Before we begin to present the 'evidence', however, we shall explain some of the ideas which contribute to our thesis, for the benefit of those who are unfamiliar with them.

Leys—a network of ancient sites

The principle behind the theory of leys is deceptively simple. It is that ancient sites of all kinds can be found to align. The sites forming such an alignment can be any combination of any of the following: stone circles, stone rows, standing stones, henges, cromlechs, hillforts, burial mounds (barrows, tumuli, cairns, etc.), ancient settlements, any other pre-Roman sites, also pre-Reformation (and sometimes later) churches and other religious buildings, and in certain circumstances also moats, prominent hills, ancient trackways, ponds, and crossroads. The minimum number of aligning sites needed before a ley can be tentatively established is disputed, but the greater the number of points there are in a short distance, the smaller is the possibility of ascribing an alignment to coincidence. Our own suggestion is that there should be at least five points within ten miles.

Initially, ley-hunting is done on an Ordnance Survey map, using a transparent straight-edge and a pencil. The most commonly used maps are the 1 inch to 1 mile (1:63,360), or, since 1974, the new maps on a scale of 1:50,000 (approximately $1\frac{1}{4}$ inches to 1 mile), depending on which you have available. (The larger scale maps have superseded the 1 inch, being published in two stages in 1974 and 1976.) Likely leys should also be checked on the $2\frac{1}{2}$-inch Ordnance Survey map (1:25,000), and then in the field.

As leys are only one of many subjects to be included in this book, there is no room to go into great detail, but the aspiring ley-hunter should read the three main books on the subject: *The Old Straight Track* by Alfred Watkins, *The View Over Atlantis* by John Michell, and *Quicksilver Heritage* by Paul Screeton. Alfred Watkins was the discoverer (or re-discoverer) of the ley system, and the 'revelation' occurred to him fifty years ago. *The Old Straight Track* did not arouse much interest when it was first published, in 1925, and for many years the subject was known to very few. Interest was rekindled on a large scale in 1969 with the publication of *The View Over Atlantis*; and the total knowledge to date has been collected together by Paul Screeton in his *Quicksilver Heritage*, published in 1974. There is also a magazine called *The Ley Hunter*, covering practical ley-hunting and the wider field of 'earth mysteries'.*

Although it is easy to find apparent alignments on Ordnance Survey maps, our experience has been that many people are not strict enough when assessing the criteria for a ley, and are also careless in their handling of both map and straight-edge. Maps are usually bought folded, and the distortions resulting from the creases can falsify the alignments. A straight-edge is easily moved, and if its position is not continually checked, it can slide away from the site marking one end of the suspected ley with the result that points appear to fall into line when in fact they do not. Another mistake made by many enthusiasts is to see a name incorporating 'ley' on the map and assume that it must mean that a ley passes through the spot. And a name ending in '–stone' or '–ston' does not necessarily indicate that

*c/o Paul Devereux, P.O. Box 152, London N10 1EP.

there were once standing stones there. To the person with a knowledge of etymology, place names can sometimes provide confirmation of a ley, but usually it is wise to disregard them in the initial stages.

Alfred Watkins concluded in print that leys marked ancient tracks, but it has been suggested that even he was not absolutely convinced that this was the true answer, because there are obvious absurdities to be explained if it was so. Leys that lead directly up steep hillsides, cross marshes, and go through ponds and rivers surely do not mark the paths over which prehistoric man travelled. Paul Screeton's book itemises the current theories and discoveries regarding leys, and what they might have been intended for—though of course the 'evidence' is tentative and unscientific if measured by Establishment standards. (It is not to the credit of academic archaeology that it invariably pays little attention to theories or areas of research which do not fit in with its accepted standards and beliefs. The attraction of cranks and slipshod workers to such fields is naturally no encouragement to the Establishment to take them seriously; but neither is it a reason for a whole subject to be rejected.)

Megalithic structures as carriers of power

Some believe that ley lines marked an energy current which flowed through the earth, and that the various mark points along a ley, standing stones, stone circles, etc., were crucial in the build-up, storage, and dispersal of this energy current. This theory is entirely alien to present-day prehistoric knowledge, for it presupposes skills in ancient man which are not only lost today, but which would generally be considered impossible for us to recover. However, if one carries in one's mind the idea that ancient sites were associated with the manipulation and storage of power or energy, one continually comes across traditions which tend to support this. There will be many such in the following chapters, but in this introductory chapter we will include a few general reports and traditions that will begin to illustrate the idea of earth currents.

Some people have experienced shocks when touching old stones, which strongly suggests that some stones carry a current of some kind. Not all people can feel them, and they are not always present. This latter feature may suggest an ebb and flow of current, possibly connected with the phases of the moon, or the positions of the planets. T. C. Lethbridge, an archaeologist who wrote several books on his experimentation with dowsing by the use of the pendulum, had an experience of this kind at the Merry Maidens stone circle, near Lamorna (Cornwall), when he was trying to ascertain the age of the circle, and he reported it in his book *The Legend of the Sons of God*:

The Merry Maidens stone circle where T. C. Lethbridge experienced 'a strong tingling sensation like a mild electric shock'.

As soon as the pendulum started to swing, a strange thing happened. The hand resting on the stone received a strong tingling sensation like a mild electric shock and the pendulum itself shot out until it was circling nearly horizontally to the ground. The stone itself, which must have weighed over a ton, felt as if it were rocking and almost dancing about. This was quite alarming, but I stuck to my counting . . . The next day I sent my wife up alone to see what happened to her. She had the same experience. It has happened nowhere else. The Pipers were mute and so were many crosses and other monuments which I have tried. But most circular monuments are now incomplete and perhaps something has gone from them.

John Williams, an experienced dowser from Abergavenny, has had similar experiences, in which he has been flung back from stones when placing his hands on them (for example, the Fish Stone near the River Usk at Penmyarth—Powys: Brecknock—and one of the Harold Stones at Trelleck, Gwent). He has described the force involved as spiral-like, building up through the whole body and throwing the person touching it back from the stone. Andrew Davidson, who uses dowsing to research into stone circles, has concentrated on a number of sites, including a stone circle in Banffshire (now Grampian) which he described during a talk to RILKO (Research into Lost Knowledge Organisation) in 1970. Through dowsing he found that each stone is predominantly positive or negative and oppositely charged to its neighbour. There are polarity changes six days after the new moon, and on one such occasion he was dowsing at the circle and experienced the change. His pendulum slowly stopped, and then gained momentum in the opposite direction, the whole sequence taking seven minutes.

It is not just individual stones which are capable of causing reactions in living creatures. Stones can also have a combined influence, and their layout is probably of great importance. The following passage from *The Witchcraft and Folklore of Dartmoor* by Ruth E. St Leger-Gordon refers to Scorhill circle on Dartmoor (Devon).

The circle has, however, acquired the reputation of being in some way eerie. I know several people who say that they are unable to ride their horses along the old track that winds right through it. Their mounts become restive and evince such unwillingness to pass inside the circumference that a detour has to be made, and the track regained on the farther side.

The horses were apparently sensitive to emanations not noticed by their riders. The literature of psychic phenomena frequently indicates that animals in general are more aware of unseen presences, and more affected by subtle influences, than most humans.

Strange effects can also be experienced at sites without stones, and a good example is described by D. A. Mac Manus in his book *The Middle Kingdom*. The unfortunate girl who fell prey to the influences of the 'fairy fort' Lis Aird, near Meelich (Mayo) was an employee of the author's aunt, and the events took place in 1935. The girl decided to climb Lis Aird one sunny afternoon, and she spent some time on the wooded summit of the hill, gazing out across the countryside. It was beginning to get chilly, so she decided to leave, and walked towards a gap in the outer bank of the earthwork. 'She had just got to the opening when she felt a queer kind of jerk, a muscular jerk inside her rather than from outside, and before she realised what had happened she found herself walking quickly in exactly the opposite direction towards the centre of the wood again.' She stopped and returned to the gap, but the same thing happened again. She naturally began to feel frightened, and decided to make for the place where she had come in over the bank. But when she tried to climb over, 'she received her greatest shock, for she felt as if an invisible wall was there which she could not pass. Whether it was all just in her mind or whether it was an invisible objective structure, she cannot to this day be sure, but it was none the less a fact that along that bank there was a line which she was quite unable to pass, unable even to stretch her arm across.' She also sensed 'with ever-growing intensity a feeling of hostility and personal resentment flooding towards her like an angry mountain stream in spate. It came, she was sure, from some point on the north-west edge of the fort, but beyond that conviction she was quite mystified.' She spent some time trying to find a way past the invisible barrier, and it began to get dark. Then she saw lanterns and heard voices calling—a search party had come to look for her. She waved and shouted, and the searchers were at one time very close, but they seemed not to see her, and eventually went away again. Now desperate, she continued to search for a way out of her prison, until suddenly she discovered that the barrier was gone, and she hurried back to the house, where she collapsed exhausted and weeping on to a settee.

The late Guy Underwood wrote an original and interesting book, which has a strong bearing on the subject of earth currents. He called it *The Pattern of the Past*, and in it he set out the results of many years' practical and theoretical research. He was a dowser, and by diligent and imaginative use of his divining rod he discovered far more than underground streams. He found a complex system of water lines and secondary patterns, to all of which he gave identifying names, calling the whole the Geodetic System. He felt strongly that the geodetic lines provided a clue to the religion of prehistory, because his investigations showed that all ancient structures mark significant geodetic features. He also felt that an unknown force was involved, the characteristics of which he outlines in this quotation from his book:

Observations of the influence which affects the water diviner suggests [*sic*] that a principle of nature exists which is unknown to, or unidentified by science. Its main characteristics are that it appears to be generated within the Earth, and to cause wave motion perpendicular to Earth's surface; that it has great penetrative power; that it affects the nerve cells of animals; that it forms spiral patterns; and is controlled by mathematical laws involving principally the numbers 3 and 7. Until it can be otherwise identified, I shall refer to it as the Earth Force. It could be an unknown principle, but it seems more likely that it is an unrecognized effect of some already established force, such as magnetism or gravity.

The Earth Force manifests itself in lines of discontinuity, which I call geodetic lines, and which form a network on the surface of the Earth. The lower animals instinctively perceive and use these lines, and their behaviour is considerably affected by them. Man is similarly affected, but less strongly, and cannot usually perceive the lines without artificial assistance.

Underwood further relates his Earth Force to the behaviour of animals—'I have found ample evidence that animals use track lines [one type of geodetic line] for finding their way, and for instinctively locating suitable places for sleeping and raising their young. These facts do something to explain why our remote ancestors set such great importance upon the Earth Force, regarding it as sacred and associated with the giving of life.'—and this tends to confirm the folklore evidence we shall present in Chapter Two, concerning the traditional rural custom of resorting to ancient sacred stones to benefit from their healing and fertilising powers, which were widely believed in. Although Underwood was primarily concerned with fieldwork and locating and plotting the geodetic lines, as the many detailed site plans in his book show, he did try to find some meaning behind the results he achieved, and what he discovered, in both practice and theory, provides further confirmation of the existence of 'earth currents'.

Why build stone circles?

It has long been believed that prehistoric monuments, especially stone circles, were originally used for rituals of some kind, but any suggestions as to the nature of the rituals have only been speculative. It seems possible that at least part of their function involved energetic dances designed to accumulate power, which was then stored in the stones—with echoes down to the present day in the witchcraft rituals sometimes performed at stone circles. T. C. Lethbridge discovered through his long experimentation with the pendulum that 'something from the human field can be fixed for long periods in the fields of various inanimate objects, including bits of stone', and his interpretation of the possible ancient use of stone circles is worth quoting.

Apparently the belief that power could be obtained by stepping up the current in human bodies is very old indeed. The stone circles, which are usually thought to be temples of some kind, are more probably places where violent dancing in a ring took place to engender power, much in the same way as in electricity a moving coil generates power. The stones were probably put there with the idea of containing the power once it had been generated. (*Witches*: Investigating an ancient religion)

Although it would probably be misleading to take the comparison with electricity too far, there are some indications that the stone circles were used for the generation of some form of current. Andrew Davidson, whom we referred to earlier, has found that the stones in one circle are alternately positively and negatively charged. With this in mind we can also note that in both the Great Circle and the Kennet Avenue at Avebury (Wiltshire) the stones are alternately a tall pillar and a diamond shape, and in view of Andrew Davidson's discovery this could possibly be more than male and female symbolism, which is the usual interpretation of these shapes. An electric current is generated by moving a conducting wire through the magnetic field that forms between the opposing poles of a magnet. A similar effect might be produced by a line of dancers weaving in and out of the stones of a circle, perhaps holding hands in order to connect their bodies together in series. By these movements they would cut through the lines of magnetic flow, and so step up the 'voltage output'. Although there remains much to be discovered about the human brain and nervous system, it seems certain that they operate on an electro-chemical basis. The rapid movement of a line of dancers in and out among the stones could have resulted in the generation of an energy which the quartz stones (frequently to be found in stone circles, as described in Chapter Six) would store or conduct into the earth. Alternatively the dance could have produced alterations in the electrical brain waves of the dancers, possibly enabling them to apprehend other levels of consciousness.

Another approach to the question of the motivation for building stone circles may be found in the works of Thom and Hawkins, whose detailed measurements and mathematics have shown that constructions such as Stonehenge, Callanish, and many stone circles could have been used as astronomical calculators. Their builders (or, more likely, a priesthood) may have calculated the future movements of the planets and stars, and one theory proposes that they would need to do this in order to have a calendar to tell them when to perform the many agricultural tasks vital to their livelihood. This may sound feasible to a town-bred scientist with little knowledge of country life. But the theory does have two serious flaws:

1. If the circles were constructed for astronomical purposes only, why was wood not used? It would have been much easier to transport, shape, and position than the tremendous pieces of stone that were often utilised. It cannot have been that there was a shortage of wood, because pollen analysis has shown that following the end of the last Ice Age trees grew thickly, even in some now windswept areas such as the Pennines and the Outer Isles. Land 2,500 feet above sea level was often forest-covered, and for some time before the end of the Bronze Age what are now inhospitable upland areas of peat bog and moorland supported settlements and cereal cultivation, indicating that the climate of the British Isles was once drier and warmer than it is now. Incidentally, the mild climate may also have

been important to the megalith builders, as well as to the farmers. The climatic deterioration coincided approximately with the beginning of the Iron Age, by which time stone monuments were no longer being built. It has been suggested that with the onset of unsettled weather, the climate was no longer suitable for the type and extent of astronomical observations carried out at stone sites, the stars, planets, and moon often being obscured at crucial moments.

2. Farmers do not sow or harvest according to a rigid calendar, but according to Nature's calendar—the natural signs of the countryside, in plants, weather, soil conditions, etc.—which varies from year to year. Many country sayings have been collected which illustrate this point, and there were apparently hundreds of them in use in past centuries. Two typical ones are:

> When the elm leaf is as big as a mouse's ear
> Then to sow barley, never fear.

> When the elm leaves are as big as a farthing, plant your beans.

Cultivation was guided by such natural signals elsewhere in the world. The American Indians advised settlers not to plant their corn until the white-oak, elm, and hickory leaves in the hills, and osage orange leaves on the plains, were as big as squirrels' ears. D. Parry-Jones, in his nostalgic book *Welsh Country Upbringing*, confirms this aspect of country life when he writes about farming in west Wales at the turn of the century:

Days counted very little in the heart of the country, hours still less, the seasons alone mattered . . . The true countryman thought and moved in seasons. There was ploughing time, sowing time, lambing time, harvest time and hiring time. He moved through life in step with the seasons, and if his thinking has tended to become slow, it is often patient, unhurried, in touch and step with deep and abiding forces.

And later:

The corn harvest was a more leisurely affair. It started at different times as the fields ripened. Certain oats were cut when they were 'the colour of the wood-pigeon' (lliw'r scythan). Farmers paid little attention to almanacs and calendars but were guided by such sayings as these which embodied the experience and the garnered wisdom of many generations. It proves how close to nature they lived and how keenly they had observed.

The detailed surveying done by Professor Alexander Thom (see bibliography) provides very positive indications that at least one function of stone circles was astronomical, but the precise calculations obtainable from these stone observatories were surely used for some purpose other than a farming calendar. It could be that the scientists of that age, by accurately plotting the positions and relationships in the heavens of the sun, moon, planets, and stars, could calculate the optimum time to capture and store the inflow of cosmic energies and the most favourable time for these energies to be released. If this should be so, then the stone circles had four mutually compatible purposes:

1. Astronomical calculators.
2. Generators of terrestrial energy.
3. Storage batteries for both cosmic and terrestrial energies.
4. Radiating devices to broadcast these energies across the land (possibly through the ley system).

Naturally constructions of stone were used because the special qualities of this material, qualities which are absent from the more easily handled wood, made it eminently suitable for storage and transmission of power.

Energies as yet undefined

If prehistoric stone structures *were* used for the purposes listed above, two vital questions are: What was the nature of the energy involved, and for what purpose was it used? The first question is the more difficult to answer, simply because so little is as yet known about the earth currents. At present we can only refer to undefined cosmic or terrestrial energies. For those who are the pioneers of the science of the coming century these energies are no less real, and their effects far more pervasive, than is electro-magnetism to the science of the twentieth century. But just as electric power, radio, and TV transmissions were matters for incredulity or derision in the late nineteenth and early twentieth centuries, so the concepts of radionics, parapsychology, and the electro force-fields of the human body meet with similar resistance from the established scientists of today, who are of the twentieth century and, understandably, cannot make use of the concepts of the twenty-first. Radionics is concerned with the balanced flow of subtle energies through the various levels of being that make man, thereby ensuring perfect health and vitality. This principle must also apply to all other living forms including our planet, which is no less alive than we are. The evidence that will follow in this book suggests that it was the original intention of early men to ensure the correctly balanced flow of life-giving energies throughout the planet and all the life forms upon it. How far they succeeded in this intention, and whether the purity of their original concept was maintained, are questions we shall examine later.

Burial mounds are frequently to be found on ley lines, and the earth currents may also have been used to assist in the transmission of the souls of the dead from this life into the next. It is questionable, however, whether prehistoric burial structures, especially the more complex megalithic tombs such as the famous passage grave at Newgrange (Meath), were built primarily to house the dead, or whether they may also have had other, more obscure, uses. Burials have undoubtedly been found in them, but burials are also present in our churches. Will archaeologists 5,000 years hence, excavating the foundations of churches and finding bones, conclude that the buildings were constructed solely to receive the dead? The possibility that megalithic tombs may have had other functions, of which traces no longer remain, should not be discarded. The small chambers within the tombs could have been used for the performance of secret rituals or ceremonies or by those seeking mystic experiences, as also could the still

Inside the fogou at Carn Euny Iron Age village (Cornwall). Just past the large stone on the right of the picture is the entrance to a small circular room which was also originally underground but is now open to the sky. Here we have experienced a strong atmosphere of peace and calm on both our visits.

enigmatic underground chambers of Cornwall and Ireland, known as fogous or souterrains, the earth-houses or weems of Scotland, and the dene-holes of Kent. Such structures, closely surrounded by earth and/or stone, sometimes roughly pyramidal in shape (for example, Maes Howe chambered tomb in Orkney), and possibly situated on leys, may have acted as a focus for the earth currents, which the occupants received in concentrated form. With this in mind, it is interesting to note that the Hopi Indians of Northern Arizona, USA, still perform their secret ceremonies in underground chambers called 'kivas'.

Some church buildings, especially cathedrals, were possibly designed to make maximum use of the currents passing through the site. There are some indications of how the power may have been controlled and used in past ages, and in this century various lone workers have attempted to re-learn the forgotten knowledge of how the shape of a construction or the shape of a volume of space can be used to concentrate the undefined energy we have been describing. Perhaps the recent experiment that has caused most interest, principally because it has caught the attention of the popular media, is the effect a pyramid shape has on the sharpness of the cutting edge of a razor blade. As reported in the widely read *Psychic Discoveries Behind the Iron Curtain* (Ostrander and Schroeder), a Czech engineer, Karel Drbal, found that by keeping a razor blade inside a correctly orientated pyramid made of cardboard, the cutting edge was retained for hundreds of shaves, owing, it was thought, to the realignment of the crystalline structure of the steel edge. (I have tried this myself and can vouch for its efficacy.—C.B.) A group in Derbyshire investigating the properties of pyramids from the religio-mystical angle constructed a pyramid large enough to accommodate a person. It was set up in the attic of a house, and the occupants claimed that they soon became aware of the 'increased energy' flowing through the rooms below. Unspecified psychic phenomena were observed in the house, and individuals sitting within the structure reported that the palms of their hands grew hot and that pulsations were felt in the region of the solar plexus. By siting a suitably shaped construction on a ley line it was perhaps possible to draw an inflow of cosmic energy down into the ley system, and many of the structures which were placed along the leys could have been designed with this object in view. The cone, which is a geometrical shape similar to that of the pyramid, is the basic shape of a church spire, many of which are noticeable features on leys; and church spires may have been the medieval equivalent of the earlier standing stones, which might themselves have been erected to facilitate the flow of energy down into the planetary body.

Degenerate rituals

A few traces remain of the rituals once performed at ancient sites. The whole question of exactly how such traditional calendar customs as Morris dancing, pace-egging, church clipping, beating the bounds, etc., derive from ancient rituals is complex. These customs are still practised at a number of ancient sites (there were many more even in the last century which have since been abandoned), and it seems almost certain that most of them have been handed down from prehistory through many generations, with their forms now much changed from the original rituals.

Clipping the church, as at Painswick (Gloucestershire) and Wirksworth (Derbyshire), means the embracing of the church by the village children, who dance hand in hand round the outside walls. Bearing in mind that churches were often built on ancient sacred sites (see Chapter Five), this may be all that remains of a rite once practised at a stone circle or standing stone which originally stood on the site. Beating the bounds may have a similar derivation, for this involves the periodic perambulation of parish boundaries. Stones often mark the limits of parishes (probably boundaries were established to pass through already existing and venerated standing stones), and at these points the children of the parish were in the past often whipped or bumped against the stones, thrown into ponds and rivers, and in other hurtful ways helped to learn the exact boundary lines. Traditional festivals like these, and those to be described in the following paragraphs, may simply mark the day on which the power flows particularly strongly through the site, or the customs practised may be the remnants of rituals which were carried out on special days in order to intensify, build up, store, or release the earth currents.

Silbury Hill (Wiltshire) was formerly visited on Palm Sunday by the people of Avebury, who celebrated there with fig cakes and sugared water. Until the beginning of this century, villagers used to climb Cley Hill near Warminster (Wiltshire) on Palm Sunday, and play a game with balls and sticks inside the prehistoric earthwork; and on the same day there was a procession to the earthwork on top of Martinsell Hill near Pewsey, also in Wiltshire. The Hove barrow (East Sussex) was the site of village games on Good Friday until its destruction in 1856; and throwl-egg (a game where dyed hard-boiled eggs were 'throwled' or rolled along the grass, the winner being the egg which rolled the farthest) was played on Shrove Tuesday at barrows near Wold Newton (North Yorkshire) and Driffield (Humberside). Early in the nineteenth century the village fair at North Thoresby (Lincolnshire) was still held near the church in a field where there was a large bluestone, around which games were played. The jury of the manorial courts formerly met at the stone. A seven-foot stone,

Silbury Hill is the largest man-made mound in Europe. Its size can be judged by comparison with the trees at its base, and the two figures standing on top.

St John's Stone, used to stand in the Abbey Fields, Leicester, and it was the custom to visit it on 24 June, St John's Day. At Durrington (Wiltshire) a fair or celebration was held on Old May Day (13 May) at the Cross Stones. A maypole with a maybush atop it was chained to the stones, and the villagers danced round the stones to a musical accompaniment, afterwards enjoying a feast of cakes and beer.

In Tayside (formerly Perthshire) on 31 October (Samhain, the eve of the Celtic New Year), a bonfire of furze was built on the Bronze Age barrow known as Carn nam Marbh (the Mound of the Dead) at Fortingall at the head of Glen Lyon. The people held hands and danced round the blazing fire, and boys ran into the fields with burning faggots. On the first day of the New Year people used to gather at a ten-foot high monolith on North Ronaldshay in the Orkneys, and there they sang and danced together. Also in Scotland, courts were held at stone circles as late as the fourteenth century, one being convened in 1349 at the standing stones of Rayne, Gairloch (Highland: Ross and Cromarty), and another at the standing stones of Easter Kyngucy in Badenach (Highland: Inverness) in 1380.

In County Cork the festival of St Kieran was celebrated by the country people at a standing stone near a ruined church dedicated to him at Cape Clear. Also in Cork there was, until about 1870, an annual fair at a ring fort at Cnocan, near Mallow, and foot-races were run alongside a barrow just outside the fort. However when the landlord transferred the fair to Ballyclough, four miles away, it died out. Many more examples of open-air meetings of all kinds being held at important local ancient sites can be found in G. L. Gomme's *Primitive Folk-Moots*.

Underground passages

The folklore of Britain abounds in stories of underground passages, few of which have been proved to exist, and most of which are physically unlikely to do so because, for example, the route crosses a river, or is several miles long. These underground passages are very strong in folk memory, and a universal fascination for secret places has probably kept these traditions alive. But since many of the tunnels are unlikely ever to have existed, where did the tales originate? The fact that all the passages appear to lead in a straight line reminds one immediately of leys, which are also straight. Are the 'underground passages' really a long-distant memory of leys? Supporting evidence for this theory is that a fair number of the underground passage stories involve treasure hidden in the tunnel—which may be a memory of the precious current within the ley line. It is not possible to prove that these traditional tales are memories of the routes of leys by tracing the underground passages on the map, because many of the ley mark points have been destroyed over the centuries. However, here are a few of the more complex traditions, involving hidden treasure, ghosts, and so on, which indicate that folk memories of underground passages are not as easy of interpretation as may at first appear.

A passage is said to run several miles from Castell Coch (the Red Castle) by the River Taff to Cardiff Castle (South Glamorgan), and at the head of the passage in Castell Coch is a cavern containing an iron chest filled with treasure. This was said to belong to Ivor the Little, Lord of Morlais, whose stronghold the castle was in the twelfth century. He had three huge eagles chained to the chest to guard the treasure, and these fierce creatures have resisted all attempts to steal it.

A treasure chest in Cleveland was also guarded by a bird, this time a raven or crow. The chest, containing gold, was said to lie in a cavern in the hills, halfway along an underground passage running from Guisborough Priory to a field in Tocketts parish.

Around sixty acres of land are enclosed by Cissbury Ring hillfort. The photograph is taken in the centre, looking towards the outer bank. The hill which is crowned by Cissbury is said to be one of the lumps of earth thrown up by the Devil when he was digging out the Devil's Dyke near Brighton (see illustration on page 95).

Cockerels guard treasure chests in two underground passages in Derbyshire: from Holmsfield Castle to Holmsfield Hall in Dronfield parish, and from Beauchief Abbey to Norton church in the same neighbourhood. The bird in each case begins to crow if anyone goes near the chest.

A West Sussex treasure hoard was guarded by large snakes which, with angry hisses, drove off anyone who started to excavate the underground passage which was said to run from Offington Hall (now demolished) to Cissbury Ring.

A ghostly monk walks above ground along the route of an underground passage four miles long from Bruern Abbey (Oxfordshire) to Tangley Hall; and a tunnel in Wiltshire, from Ivy church to the Green Dragon inn at Alderbury, is said to be haunted, possibly by monks.

A strange story is told of several underground passages, including: (1) Old Grange (a ruin near Cinderford, Gloucestershire) to Flaxley Abbey; (2) Malling Abbey (or Leybourne Grange) to Smuggler's Cave on top of the Downs at Ryarsh (Kent); (3) Binham Priory to Walsingham Abbey (Norfolk). Halfway along all these routes is a small wood called Fiddler's Copse, and this name commemorates the story of a fiddler who walked along the passage playing his fiddle while his brother followed above ground, listening. (They were trying to discover where the passage led.) In all cases, the sound of fiddling ceased beneath the copse, and the fiddler was never seen again. A variation on this story comes from St Mary's in the Scilly Isles. Piper's Hole, a pool of fresh water at the foot of the headland called Peninnis, is said to be the entrance to an undersea passage leading to another Piper's Hole on the island of Tresco. People who entered were never seen again—they were overcome by fatigue, the passage being too narrow for them to turn round and return. Dogs which entered the passage were luckier; they were seen to emerge many days later from the hole on Tresco, though emaciated and almost hairless. There is no mention of musical explorers, but the name 'Piper's Hole' suggests that at one time this passage had some version of the fiddler story associated with it.

Traditions of underground passages are widespread throughout Britain, but fairy paths seem to be peculiar to Ireland (though it may well be that they were known on this side of the Irish Sea before fairies became scarce). Like underground passages, these paths also sound like degenerate memories of leys, and the recorded effects of interfering with them certainly support this possibility. An old schoolmaster living in western County Limerick and writing in 1943 (quoted in Kevin Danaher's *The Year in Ireland*) commented:

It was widely believed that a house built on a path frequented by the fairies and other such uncanny travellers would suffer from midnight noises or supernatural manifestations. Perhaps too, ill-luck in the farm or personal illness etc.

might afflict the family. One remedy for these evils was to bring on St John's Eve portions of the blessed fire [which was lit every year at sunset on 23 June] and to build with them on the path in several places small fires which would be left burning until morning.

A graphic demonstration of the inadvisability of obstructing a fairy path is given in the following story. The events related took place in the 1930s, and the author of *The Middle Kingdom* (where the details come from) did not identify people or places because at the time of his writing the story 'is too poignant'. A family was experiencing a great deal of sorrow because, one after another, four children sickened and died, leaving doctors baffled. The fifth child became ill and was near death, and so the doctor was amazed when the child's father hurried to tell him that the boy was well again—and that there would be no more deaths. Apparently, the father had gone to a wise woman to see if she could throw any light on the tragedies, and she immediately saw what was wrong. A few months before the first illness, the father had built an extension to his house, but this was badly placed for it 'just obtruded into a straight line between two neighbouring fairy forts'. The wise woman advised him to demolish the extension, which he did the same night, and then found that the dying child was much improved. This tale also illustrates the importance attached to the correct siting of buildings, a subject which will be returned to in Chapter Five in especial relation to churches.

The fairies of Ireland are not the only people to follow straight paths. Evidence for similar traditions has been found in other parts of the world, including Australia where the Aborigines have preserved the sacred paths crossing their tribal homelands. Their mythology tells that these paths were the routes their supernatural ancestors took at the dawn of time, and at certain points there were magical centres where sacred rites were performed, these journeys and ritual acts being re-enacted by the Aborigines. Alan Cohen's description of this in *The Ley Hunter* (no. 34) shows how close their concepts are to what is believed to lie behind the ley system:

By following the sacred paths they would remind themselves that their entire landscape was constructed according to a divine pattern; by performing increase rituals at the magic centres they would activate the sleeping life-power intrinsic to those sites, and thus fertilise the whole countryside.

Buried treasure

Treasure hoards were touched upon in the previous section on underground passages, and mention was made of the possibility that the treasure was in fact the 'ley power' or earth current. Possible support for this comes

This stone cist on the eastern side of Rillaton barrow contained a skeleton, a bronze dagger, and a gold cup. After excavation in 1818, the cup (*below*) was lost for a time, then rediscovered in King George V's dressing room at Buckingham Palace where it had found its way as treasure trove. On the horizon, a knob on the left-hand side of the hill is the Cheesewring, which features in Chapter Six.

in the form of many accounts of treasure buried within the area of ancient structures, especially burial mounds. Again some of these tales may indicate a distant memory of the power inherent in the site. Many of the traditions have been proved *factually* false, in that no treasure has been found, but occasionally the memory has been verified and treasure unearthed. This supports our argument that folk memory is not as unreliable as many people believe, and that the content of handed-down traditions often has some foundation in fact.

Two examples of verified folk memory come from Clwyd and Cornwall. The ghost of a huge man dressed in gold was said to haunt a barrow called Bryn yr Ellyllon (Hill of the Goblins) at Mold (Clwyd: Flint). When the barrow was opened in 1833, a gold corselet or cape was discovered (which is now in the British Museum). The Rillaton barrow on Bodmin Moor (Cornwall) also had a ghost story. The ghost was of a druid priest who used to sit in the rocky Druid's Chair nearby and offer passers-by a drink of a magic potion from a gold cup which no one could drain. A drunken hunter threw the dregs in the ghost's face; shortly afterwards he and his horse were found dead in a ravine, and he was buried still holding the cup. In 1818 a skeleton and a gold beaker (also now in the British Museum) were discovered during excavations in the barrow.

Traditions of buried treasure are still current at the following ancient sites (and many others):

BERKSHIRE
Round barrow at Beedon—gold or silver coffin.
Barrow near Great Shefford—gold.
Barrow on Inkpen Hill—gold table.

CAMBRIDGESHIRE
Mutlow Hill, Great Wilbraham—golden coach.

CLWYD
Cairn on Nerquis Mountain (Flintshire)—chest of gold (not found during late nineteenth-century excavation).
Cerrig y Drudion (Denbighshire)—gold chest.

CORNWALL
Carne Beacon near Veryan—Gerennius, a mythical king of Cornwall, in a golden boat with silver oars. (Opened 1855, but only a stone chest containing ashes was found.)
Men Scryfa near Madron—a man who dug for the gold reputedly hidden beneath this inscribed stone only succeeded in uprooting the stone (now restored).

Trencrom Hill near St. Ives—the giants who lived in the Iron Age hillfort hid their treasure inside the hill. '200 years ago' a tin miner, seeing lights on the hill one night, crept up and saw a long passage down which was the unguarded treasure. He took some of the gold and used it to buy land. Another story tells of a man who dug for gold on the hill, until frightened away by a tremendous storm, plus the arrival of countless numbers of spriggans (the trolls who protected the giants' gold), looking 'as ugly as if they would eat him'.

St Michael's Mount can be seen from the top of Trencrom Hill, whose slopes are littered with large boulders. There is nothing to be seen of the giants' treasure, however, or of the spriggans who guard it.

This overgrown tumulus at St Weonard's is said to be the burial place of a saint.

DEVON
Simon's Barrow, on Blackdown, Hemyock—crock of gold.
Wood Barrow, Challacombe—brass pan full of gold and silver.

FIFE
Norrie's Law—it was said that this barrow was so rich in gold the sheep's fleeces turned yellow when they lay on it. In 1819 when sand was being dug from the mound (is this the 'gold' in the sheep's coats?), armour, a shield, a sword handle, and silver scabbard were found.

HEREFORD AND WORCESTER
Tumulus near the church at St Weonard's—St Weonard in a golden coffin on top of a golden coffer filled with gold.

HUMBERSIDE
Willy Howe round barrow—treasure.

LINCOLNSHIRE
A large boulder in Digby parish—much treasure buried beneath this boulder. (But it would be very difficult for prospective treasure-seekers to locate, because the boulder has now 'buried itself'!)

The Long Man of Wilmington, 225 feet tall, is a chalk-cut figure of uncertain age and parentage.

POWYS

Y Garn Coch near Ystradgynlais (Brecknock)—three cauldrons full of gold.

SURREY

Tolt Hill near Hambledon—treasure.

SUSSEX

Many sites along the South Downs and close by are said to contain treasure, for example: in West Sussex—Pulborough Mount, The Trundle (Golden Calf), and Chanctonbury Ring; in East Sussex—Clayton Hill (Golden Calf), Firle Beacon (silver coffin), Hollingbury Camp, Mount Caburn (silver coffin, and a knight in golden armour), and the Long Man of Wilmington (a Roman in a golden coffin).

WILTSHIRE
Winkelbury Hill, Berwick St John—golden coffin.
Round barrow at Enford—golden chair.
Barrow Lane, Littleton Drew—golden wheelbarrow.
Silbury Hill—a king in a golden coffin/a man in golden armour on horseback.

Stories of hidden treasure are also told about other sites not obviously prehistoric, and investigation might show that such sites are on leys, for example Stokesay Castle (Salop), Bronsil Castle, Penyard Castle, and Longtown Castle (all Hereford and Worcester), Alcock's Arbour near Haselor (Warwickshire), Broomlee Lough (Northumberland), and in Snodhill Park in Golden Valley (Hereford and Worcester), where a vast treasure is said to lie buried 'no deeper than a hen could scratch'.

Fecundity

Some traditions have fertility and fecundity as their main themes, and they may reflect the beneficial influence of the earth currents which were once widespread throughout the land. A complex fecundity tradition involves mysterious cows which can give an endless supply of milk. The best-known tale is that of the White Cow of Mitchell's Fold (a stone circle in Salop). In a time of famine this pure white cow could be found night and morning at the stone circle, ready for milking. She allowed each person a pailful; if anyone were to take more, she would never return. A spiteful old witch milked the cow into a sieve, which of course she could not fill, and finally the witch milked her dry. The cow never returned, and the witch was punished by being turned into what is now the tallest stone in the ruined circle. Variations on this story tell that the witch was buried in the middle of the circle, to prevent her from reappearing as a ghost; that the cow belonged to a giant who used to milk her; and that the cow was not milked dry, but saw what was happening in a flash of lightning, kicked the witch (who remained rooted to the spot), and vanished.

There is a similar white cow legend on Lewis (Western Isles). She appeared in the sea when there was famine in the island, and told a woman who was intent on drowning herself to go home and fetch her milk pail, and the neighbours with theirs, and take them to the stones of Callanish.

All had their pails filled with milk, and the cow provided each person with one pailful every night. But a witch who tried unsuccessfully to get two pails of milk from the cow returned the next night with a pail which had a sieve for its bottom, and she milked the cow dry. It was never seen again at the Callanish stones.

A huge dun cow used to wander over the Lancashire moors of Parlick, Bleasdale, Bowland, and Browsholme. She too gave plenty of milk, but was eventually milked dry by a witch. She was buried in Cow Hill, Grimsargh, near Preston, and it is said that large bones have been discovered there. An enormous rib, said to be from the dun cow, was placed over the door of the 'Old Rib' farmhouse in the township of Whittingham, near Preston.

Another dun cow legend comes from Stanion (Northamptonshire),

Open moorland close to the England/Wales border was the territory of one of Britain's legendary milch cows, the White Cow of Mitchell's Fold. The stones here belong to the stone circle where she is said to have been milked dry, and the tall stone on the right may be the petrified witch who thus ill-treated her.

whose church houses a bone nearly six feet long reputedly belonging to the animal. (This and similar huge bones are probably whale bones, which obviously had a high curiosity value when they were brought into the country.) Again, a witch milked her into a sieve, and she died of exhaustion. The Dun Cow of Warwick was another which was milked dry by a witch: she became a man-eater as a result, and was killed by Guy of Warwick, a legendary tenth-century hero. A bone in the Foljambe Chapel, Warwick, seven feet four inches long, is said to be one of her ribs.

In Wales, Y Fuwch Frech, the freckled cow, lived on Hiraethog Mountain near Cerrigydrudion (Clwyd: Denbigh). On being milked into a sieve by a witch, she drowned herself in Llyn Dau Ychen. A legend in the Welsh *Iolo MSS*, with the title 'Y Fuwch Laethwen Lefrith' (The Milk-White Milch Cow), tells of another cow with bountiful supplies of milk, and she almost suffered the ultimate humility at the hands of the Welsh:

The milk-white milch cow gave enough of milk to every one who desired it; and however frequently milked, or by whatever number of persons, she was never found deficient. All persons who drank of her milk were healed of every illness; from being fools they became wise; and from being wicked, became happy. This cow went round the world and wherever she appeared, she filled with milk all the vessels that could be found, leaving calves behind her for all the wise and happy. It was from her that all the milch cows in the world were obtained. After traversing the island of Britain, for the benefit and blessing of country and kindred, she reached the Vale of Towy; where, tempted by her fine appearance and superior condition, the natives sought to kill and eat her; but just as they were proceeding to effect their purpose, she vanished from between their hands, and was never seen again. A house still remains in the locality, called Y Fuwch Laethwen Lefrith.

Perhaps the milk which provided fruitfulness and happiness for all symbolised the earth currents which were used in the past to maintain the wellbeing and prosperity of the people. But when the witch milked the cow into a sieve, i.e. too much of the life-giving current was taken from the system, total disruption occurred and the flow ceased altogether.

Despite the local unpopularity of the county boundary and name changes instituted in 1974 and 1975, we have bowed to the winds of change and incorporated the new names into our text. In the case of Wales and Scotland, however, where three or more old counties have often been amalgamated into one new county or region, we also give the relevant old county name, so that the location of the site can be more easily pinpointed than would have been the case had we only given the name of a vast new county. In England there are no huge new counties, so the problem does not arise.

This book is not intended as a guide to the sites we describe, and we do not know that all the sites are still in existence. This applies especially to standing stones, which are often moved by famers because they obstruct the giant machines used nowadays. All our own photographs are recent, and those sites still survive; as for the others, the use in our text of the present tense does not guarantee that you will find the site if you go and look for it, for many of our sources are a hundred or more years old. You may well find it, for these old relics have a tendency to endure despite the twentieth-century mania for change, though it may be in a sorry state; but don't blame us if no trace of it remains!

It was written in *The New Statistical Account of Scotland* (1843–4) concerning the Borestone at Trinity Gask (Tayside: Perth): 'There are many traditions and legends connected with this relic, but they are too absurd to be committed to writing.' We do not subscribe to this attitude, and we hope that our book will show it to be a shortsighted approach to the ancient sites and their traditions.

2   Stones and their powers

The Countless Stones (Lower Kit's Coty House) are all that remains of a Neolithic burial chamber.

It would seem as if the hidden current which flows through the land can be tapped at certain points, much as an electric socket on the skirting board of our sitting room enables us to 'plug in' to the current and put it to use. These outlets are thought to exist at ancient sites and particularly in the huge blocks of stone which were erected as circles or single standing stones by the ancient race who must originally have gathered, channelled, and used the earth currents. The many traditions attached to stones and relating to cures and fertility testify to the beneficent effects of these currents, when correctly applied and controlled by the human mind.

Up until very recent times the old stones have usually been treated with respect and veneration by the people in their locality, and many of the surviving practices indicate a distorted knowledge of a power that once was of the utmost concern to the populace, and through which natural forces could be controlled and manipulated for the benefit of all living creatures. Of the King Stone, a sinuous monolith standing isolated in a field on the opposite side of the road from the Rollright Stones (Oxfordshire), Arthur J. Evans reported in *Folk-Lore* in 1895 that 'Chips were taken from the King Stone for "good luck" and by soldiers "to be good for England in battle" . . . the Welsh drovers who used to trench the road with their cattle before the railway was made, used continually to be chipping off pieces, so that formerly the stone was much bigger than it is now'. This 'souvenir hunting' was probably the final phase before all knowledge of the stone's history and significance was forgotten and it became merely an archaeological curiosity. Attached to the Rollright Stones themselves is the tradition of the baker who, wishing to count the stones, placed a loaf of bread on each stone, but was thwarted in his attempt to ascertain the number of these countless stones, because a loaf was missing each time he counted, or, in another version, his supply of loaves was insufficient. A baker used the same technique to try and count the stones of Lower Kit's Coty House in Kent, but with no more success. Three possible explanations have been given for his failure: the Devil appeared in place of one of the loaves; the Devil ate some of the loaves and then sat gibbering at the discomfited baker; the baker fell dead as he was on the point of announcing the number of stones. A similar tradition was also attached to Stonehenge (Wiltshire), of which Daniel Defoe wrote in his *Tour Through England and Wales* (1724): 'a baker carry'd a basket of bread, and laid a loaf upon every stone, [presumably he also used a ladder—or did he place them at the base?] and yet could never make out the same number twice'. These stories may stem from the memories of food offerings that were made to the stones long ago. Of the Hurlers (a group of three stone circles on Bodmin Moor, Cornwall), it was written by Dr Yonge in 1675 that they are 'now easily numbered but the people have a story that they never could till a man took many penny Loafes and laying one on each hurler did compute by the rem^d what number they were'. This was a rare success: the countless stones usually remained so, two examples of the dozen or more in England being Long Meg and Her Daughters (Cumbria) and the circles at Stanton Drew (Avon).

Other examples of offerings to stones are found in Scotland, where until the early years of this century libations were poured into cup markings and natural hollows in stones. Daily at the Stone of the Long-Haired One (Clach-na-Gruagach) in Gairloch (Highland: Ross and Cromarty) an offering of milk was poured into a hollow in the stone, and, referring to the parish of Kilmuir in Skye (Highland), *The New Statistical Account for Scotland* reported in 1842:

Some time ago the natives firmly believed in the existence of the Gruagach, a female spectre of the class of Brownies, to whom the dairy-maids made frequent libations of milk. The Gruagach was said to be an innocent supernatural visitor . . . Even so late as 1770, the dairy-maids, who attended a herd of cattle in the island of Trodda, were in the habit of pouring daily a quantity of milk in a hollow stone for the Gruagach. Should they neglect to do so they were sure of feeling the effects of the Brownie the next day. It is said that the Rev Donald MacQueen, the then minister of this Parish, went purposely to Trodda to check that gross superstition. He might then have succeeded for a time in doing so, but it is known that many believed in the Gruagach's existence long after that reverend gentleman's death.

On the island of Westray in the Orkneys milk was poured into a hole in the centre of one of two tumuli known as Wilkie's Knolls. It was said that if this offering were to be neglected Wilkie would send pestilence upon the cattle. The cattle on an islet off Benbecula (Western Isles) suffered when a new dairymaid was employed who refused to continue the old custom of 'spilling a coggie of milk on the fairy-knoll'. The best cow died, and the others gave blood not milk; so the previous dairymaid was hurriedly fetched back and all was well again. This story came from an old shepherd whose grandfather had been the cowherd on the islet at the time.

In Ireland, blood rather than milk was used in a custom which has sacrificial echoes. On May Eve, according to the *Ulster Journal of Archaeology* (1855, 165), 'the peasantry used to drive all their cattle into old raths and forts thought to be much frequented by the fairies, bleed them, taste their blood, and pour the remainder on the earth'.

Offerings left at stones took a number of forms. 'La Gran'mère du Chimquière' is a menhir roughly carved into a female shape, with a face, drapery, and exposed breasts, which stands in the churchyard of St Martin-de-la-Beilleuse on Guernsey (Channel Islands), and it was thought to be lucky to place an offering of spirits before her. Even as late as the 1920s, the rector found bunches of flowers and other small offerings at her feet. In County Limerick, the largest stone in the stone circle at Grange by Lough Gur used to be garlanded with flowers.

At midnight, when there was a full moon, maidens from the Swansea district used to leave cakes of barley-meal, honey, and milk on Arthur's Stone, which stands on Cefn-y-Bryn, Gower (West Glamorgan). They then crawled round the stone three times on hands and knees, hoping to see their sweethearts. If they appeared, their fidelity was proved. If not, then the girls knew that the boys did not intend to marry them.

Perhaps the most striking instance of a sacrificial offering being made to an ancient stone occurred at Holne (Devon) up until the early years of this century. Here on May Day morning a live ram was tied to a granite menhir which stands in the centre of Ploy Field; its throat was cut, and the blood allowed to flow over the stone. Then the whole animal, wool and hide too, was roasted, and slices of meat, considered to bring good luck, were scrambled for. The day ended with dancing, games, and wrestling.

The practices just described, and indeed most of the traditions in this book, indicate a veneration for the ancient sites, and especially standing stones. This is illustrated very clearly in the following story. In the 'Field of the Bowing' near Galtrigal, Isle of Skye (Highland), used to stand the Bowing Stone. People would come especially to walk round it three times

The standing stones of Callanish.

and bow, for it was the stone of the ancient gods and to bow to it would ensure a good harvest. Then came to the area a minister who did not approve of the people worshipping a pagan idol, and he had the stone removed to the churchyard, but the people still bowed to it, so he had it thrown into a field. The farmer whose land it now lay on was annoyed when his crops were trampled by people visiting the stone, so he got his sons to throw it into a ravine. A sheriff learned of this and ordered them to replace it, but they found it was broken. So they collected the pieces and piled them up, and the people still came to bow. Not far away, on Lewis (Western Isles), the standing stones of Callanish were held in awe by the local families, and up until late in the last century it was the custom to visit the stones secretly, at Midsummer and on May Day especially. The visits were made openly until condemned by the Church ministers, after which time they were made in secret, 'for it would not do to neglect the Stones'.

This veneration of ancient stones and earthworks can therefore be seen as the last lingering acknowledgement of the power and importance of these sites for the welfare of the community, though the practices described above were surely far removed from the original manipulations of energy that occurred, and the origins of the latterday celebrations were a closed book to their participants. Tradition decreed that respect be paid to these ancient monoliths, though the people knew not how or why, and so, in their simple fashion, they peopled the stones with spirits and sought to placate them with offerings of food and animal sacrifices.

Healing stones

There are a great number of traditions relating to the use of stones for healing purposes, and it seems clear that such traditions embody ancient practices based on the skilled use of the energies accumulated in the stones. As with most of the types of tradition described in this book, stones with the power to cure were to be found in other parts of Europe, and the antiquity of these customs is illustrated by the fact that a number of edicts were passed between AD 450 and 1100, mostly in France and Spain, prohibiting visits to stones for the cure of disease.

In the British Isles holed stones seem to have been considered particularly potent, especially in effecting cures for children, and probably the most famous example is the Men-an-Tol near Madron in Cornwall. The Men-an-Tol is a wheel-shaped stone with a central hole about two feet in diameter and it stands upright between two standing stones. Prevention and cure of a variety of illnesses of a rheumatic nature could be obtained by crawling through the holed stone or, in the case of an infant, passing the baby through the stone following a certain sequence of actions. For ex-

The two stones flanking the Men-an-Tol (stone of the hole) are known to have been moved from their original positions. All three stones are thought to have once formed part of a Neolithic burial chamber.

ample, scrofulous children were passed naked through the stone three times and then drawn three times along the grass in an easterly direction. Adults seeking relief, especially from ague, were advised to crawl through the hole nine times against the sun: the stone would 'blacken disease' and sufferers would be cured of any 'ailment or nightmare or weight in your chest'.

In Ireland, in the parish of Aghade (Carlow), the Cloch-a-Phoill is a large, semi-recumbent stone seven and a half feet tall with a hole eleven and a half inches in diameter; children were passed through the hole to prevent or cure rickets. Also in Ireland, there is a stone known variously as the Speckled Stone (Clochbhreac) and the Gray Stone (Clochlia) because of its mottled appearance. It is in County Sligo, at Tobernavean, Woodville, near Sligo, and at the junction of three parishes. This limestone flag is set on edge and measures ten feet broad by nine feet high. It has in it a perforation three feet by two feet, and in earlier years children with measles and other maladies were passed through the aperture to obtain a cure. Similarly at the Long Stone, Minchinhampton (Gloucestershire), children with measles, whooping cough, and other diseases were passed through a perforation in the stone.

There is a holed stone in Devon, in the North Teign River on Dartmoor, called the Tolmen (*tol* = hole, *maen* = stone). It is a large boulder in the river bed, and the hole was presumably worn by the friction of the water. Those who can climb on to the rock and drop through unscathed on to the stone slab below will thenceforth be immune to all rheumatic complaints—but this procedure is not advisable when the river is in full spate!

A holed stone in Brahan Wood, Dingwall (Highland: Ross and Cromarty) was, until early this century, thought to have healing powers, and sick children were taken there for a cure, first their clothing and then the children themselves being passed through the hole. Donald A. Mackenzie gives first-hand evidence of the local belief in the healing power of this stone in his book *Scottish Folk-Lore and Folk Life*:

Until recently it was the custom to take ailing children to this holed rock so that they might be cured. A fire was lit and the clothing of a stripped child was passed through the hole from one woman to another and then the child was passed through.

When a member of a family was seriously ill a woman baked cakes at the holed rock and, having fired them on a stone placed in proximity to a wood fire, left them on the summit of the rock. If by next morning they had vanished it was believed that the patient would recover, but if they remained it was feared that the patient would die. A young south country doctor who was acting as a 'locum' to a Dingwall doctor about twenty years ago [*c.* 1915] attended a patient not far from the holed rock. On his second visit he found that the illness had taken a serious turn and he spoke gravely to the patient's mother, who puzzled him greatly by remarking, 'He is sure to recover, doctor; the cakes were taken last night'. The southerner was puzzled and asked what she meant. 'Oh! it's just a saying we will have,' came the evasive answer. The doctor consulted the writer, who suspected that the reference was to a folk custom, and he ultimately discovered that the cake-divination custom was often practised by women, assisted by children, who gathered dry sticks for the fire but were sent away before the cakes were baked and deposited. The local clergymen, doctors and school teachers and even the husbands of some of the women guilty of perpetuating the pagan custom were quite unaware of it.

Small holed stones also had their uses, for they had the advantage that they could be carried to wherever they were needed, and in Suffolk the belief was held that a holed stone tied to the head of the bed would prevent nightmares. In East Anglia, Yorkshire, and Ireland holed flints known as 'hag-stones' or 'ring-stones' were hung in the stable or cowshed, to stop witches from hag-riding the horses or harming the cows and stealing their milk. In County Antrim, hollow stones were hung round the necks of cows, presumably to protect them from illness and evil. Holed stones worn by the sick in the New Forest area of Hampshire were exposed beforehand to the rays of the full moon for three nights.

Rocks which appeared to be of natural formation but which had an opening below through which a person could crawl were also considered to be effective in promoting cures. There is on the shore at Ardmore in County Waterford a rock with a small natural arch on its underside. This is the Cloch-Nave-Deglane, and the rite of passing three times under the stone to obtain relief from backache has been incorporated into the Christian observances which pilgrims practised on the festival of St Declan on 22 December. In 1833 an eye-witness wrote:

The greater part of the strand on the west side of Ardmore Bay was literally covered by a dense mass of people . . . The devotional exercises were commenced at an early hour, by passing under the holy rock of St. Declan in a state of half-nudity. Stretched at full length on the ground on his face and stomach, each devotee moved forward, as if in the act of swimming, and thus they squeezed or dragged their bodies through. Both sexes were obliged to submit to this humiliating mode of proceeding. Upwards of 1,100 persons were observed to go through this ceremony in the course of the day . . . After working their way through, all rose on their knees and struck their backs three times against the stone, removing beads and repeating aves all the while. They then proceeded on bare knees over a number of little rocks to the place where they had to enter again under the stone, and thus proceeded three times, which done they washed their knees, bodies and dress and made for the well . . . The priests had vainly tried to put an end to the practices here described, even whipping the people from St. Declan's stone, but it was impossible to stop the old custom of the people.

Similar healing stones are also found in Cornwall and Grampian. The stone known as the Cornish Pebble, at Perranarworthal in Cornwall, is balanced upon two supporting stones, and was said to cure the sciatica and rheumatism of those who were prepared to crawl round it on all fours during the month of May, sunwise, east to west, and squeeze through the aperture. In the parish of Fyvie (Grampian: Aberdeen) there is a large stone supported on two others under which mothers passed their sick children. (The large number of traditions relating to the curing of *child-*

It cannot have been easy to pass children over the top of the Drake Stone, and it is to be hoped that those who tried this cure had their efforts rewarded.

ren's ailments illustrates the high incidence of illness in the young in earlier centuries.)

Another variation on the holed stone is the forked rock, such as the Crick Stone at Morva (Cornwall). Those who could pass through the fork yet not touch the stone would certainly be cured of 'crick in the back'. This same belief is attached to other groups of rock in Cornwall which appear to have been formed by natural falls leaving a small opening through which a person could pass. Certain stones without holes or apertures of any kind were also credited with curative properties. Simply to pass three times between the King Stone and Queen Stone on Bredon Hill (Hereford and Worcester) was considered sufficient to cure all ills, while on the island of Islay (Strathclyde) the Stone of the Toothache could cure a sufferer of that painful affliction if he drove a nail into the stone. On Harbottle Crags in Northumberland, sick children were passed over the top of the tall Drake Stone. The belief in its power to cure must have been strong, because this is a massive block of sandstone, and to pass sick children over it must have been quite a feat. Perhaps there was an attempt at moral control by a Christian priest near Nancledra in Cornwall, because the Twelve O'Clock Stone was believed to cure children of rickets, so long as they were not illegitimate or their parents of a dissolute nature.

The power in the stones could also be conveyed to the human frame by physical contact (see also 'Inauguration stones' later in this chapter). Near Comrie in Tayside (Perthshire) is St Fillan's Chair, which is a seat formed in the natural rock on Dunfillan Hill and is the place from which the saint blessed the neighbourhood. Here was a cure for rheumatism of the spine: the afflicted had to climb the rock and sit in the chair and then be pulled down the hillside by the ankles (kill or cure tactics!). A similar seat is located in Dyfed (Carmarthenshire), in a field adjoining the old church of Llangan. This seat is associated with the nearby well of Ffynon Canna and is known as Canna's Stone. It was effective in curing ague, and those seeking relief would sit on the stone, and preferably sleep on it, after drinking the well waters. This procedure was intended to be continued for several days, and even weeks. On Ben Newe, Strathdon (Grampian: Aberdeen), is a rock basin which as late as the eighteenth century was, according to a manuscript of that time, 'renowned among the vulgar for marvellous cures; there is said to be a worm abiding in it, which, if alive when the patient comes, he or she will live; if dead they are condemned to die'. This 'worm' which can be either alive or dead may be an uncomprehending description of the power in the stone which is known to fluctuate: if active when the stone is visited, a cure can be obtained; if quiescent, then the sufferer is out of luck.

Other stones, not necessarily large, fixed, or holed, were also considered to have powers of curing illness. The value of this group of stones was that they could be passed from one person to another, and used privately by the afflicted. Such a one could be found in Ireland and was kept near St Conall's Well by Donegal Bay. This stone was dark brown and dumbbell-shaped, but only five inches long. Ailing people had this stone brought to their houses, where it was kept until they regained their health. Then the stone was returned to its resting place in the hollow of a broken cross at 'The Relig', which is near Bruckless on the north side of Donegal Bay. No one had the duty of custodian for this marvellous healing stone, but when it was borrowed the people living nearby were informed and it was returned after use without question. It is said that it had travelled as far afield as America, where a local person who had emigrated there had need of it.

Another portable healing stone in Ireland was to be found at Dromatimore (Cork), close by St Olan's Well. It was called St Olan's Cap, and

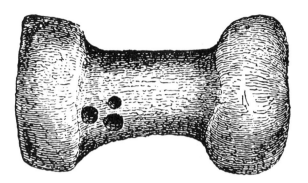

The healing stone of St Conall.

rested atop St Olan's Stone, a monolith inscribed with ogham characters. The original Cap was removed by the parish priest over a century ago and replaced by an oval quartzite stone, though whether in shape and type of stone the new one exactly duplicated the old is not clear. The original Cap 'was said to be an unfailing talisman, and was much sought after for various feminine ailments, particularly maternity cases. If worn on the head and carried three times round the church it was said to cure the most violent headaches and, in addition, it had the gift of locomotion in that, if removed to any distance, it unfailingly returned to its original position.' (P. J. Harnett, *Béaloideas*, 10 (1941), 103). More examples of stones which return when removed are given in Chapter Eight.

In some other parts of the British Isles, stones from Ireland were most favoured for healing purposes. In the Stamfordham area of Northumberland there was such a stone which was never permitted to touch English ground. When needed it was conveyed to the sufferer in a basket and then rubbed on the part of the body that was injured, whereupon the wound would very quickly heal. It was, however, considered to be most effective in the hands of an Irish person. Scotland too had its portable healing stones, for example the stitch-stones of Highland (Ross and Cromarty) which could be used to cure all manner of ailments from sciatica to pleurisy. These stones were kept by the last person to use them until someone else had need of them, when they were passed on. The Reverend K. Macdonald of Applecross, writing about stitch-stones in his *Social and Religious Life in the Highlands*, says:

The last specimen of which I heard about 30 years ago [*c.* 1872] was in Erradale, parish of Gairloch. Mr. Matheson, Free Church minister, got hold of it and took it to the pulpit one day. At the close of the service he held it up before the congregation, remarking that the god of Erradale was the smallest god of which he had ever heard or read. It was a small piece of flint stone, 3 or 4 in. long,

The Clach Dearg or Red Stone belonged to the Campbells of Ardvorlich (Tayside: Perth) and was used for curing distemper in cattle and humans, who drank water in which the stone had been dipped.

found on the shore and highly polished by the action of the waves . . . Mr. Matheson broke it in their presence, and yet no dire results followed.

The use of a liquid as a means of conveying the potency from stone to patient was not uncommon. The waters of Loch Monar in the Scottish Highlands were said to have healing properties. The story is that a woman who lived nearby possessed some charmed pebbles, which when placed in water could impart their virtue to the liquid. Once when she was out walking there was an attempt to rob her of these stones, but she evaded her attacker and, running to the lake, she threw the stones into it. From that time the lake was endowed with miraculous healing powers, especially on the first Mondays in November, February, May, and August. (It is significant that the first days of these months mark the festivals which started the four seasons in the Celtic calendar, i.e. Samhain, Oimelc, Beltane, and Lugnasad respectively.) In order to take advantage of the powers the pilgrims had to gather on the bank at midnight, plunge three times into the water, drink a little, and throw in a coin as an offering. If the treatment was to be completely effective, they had to be well out of sight of the loch by sunrise.

On Lewis (Western Isles), where cattle diseases were considered to be the result of serpent bites, the cattle were given water into which charm stones had been placed. The FitzGerald family (location not known) have been the guardians of the Imokilly amulet for many generations, and water into which this five-ounce agate had been dipped was considered a cure for murrain or hydrophobia, hence its more common name the 'murrain stone'. In 1895 the owner was still able to say, 'Even at present, many apply to me for it.' The owner of a marble-sized crystal at Liscarrol (Cork) used to dip it into water once a year and give the water to the local farmers who had gathered to witness the ceremony. What they used it for was not recorded.

Layamon (*fl.* 1200), priest, historian, and poet, described Stonehenge in his great poem *Brut*:

> The stones are great
> And magic power they have
> Men that are sick
> Fare to that stone
> And they wash that stone
> And bathe away their evil.

The giant structure of Stonehenge (Wiltshire) was considered to have great healing virtue, as is shown by Geoffrey of Monmouth, who in his *History of the Kings of Britain* quotes Merlin's reply to King Aurelius's amused query regarding Stonehenge:

'Laugh not so lightly, King, for not lightly are these words spoken. For in these stones is a mystery, and a healing virtue against many ailments. Giants of old did carry them from the furthest ends of Africa and did set them up in Ireland what time they did inhabit therein. And unto this end they did it, that they might make them baths therein whensoever they ailed of any malady, for they did wash the stones and pour forth the water into the baths, whereby they that were sick were made whole. Moreover, they did mix confections of herbs with the water, whereby they that were wounded had healing, for not a stone is there that lacketh in virtue of leechcraft.'

Before we turn from healing to fertility, it is relevant to consider why such a variety of stones are credited with the power of curing sickness. We have described holed stones shaped by prehistoric man, natural holed stones, small holed stones which are portable, stones with apertures beneath, forked stones, large stones apparently with no special visible characteristics, stone seats, and small stones only inches long which often need to be used second-hand, that is, water in which they have been immersed is used to effect a cure. The theory that earth currents were used in the healing process can only be applied to large stones in contact with the earth. The traditions connected with these stones are straightforward in that they all involve a ritual through which an intake of energy occurs, by the afflicted person either passing through a hole or in some other way coming into close contact with the stone and thereby being affected by its force-field and receiving the health-giving earth current.

But what of the small stones not in contact with the earth, and which therefore cannot be considered part of the earth currents network? In Chapter Six we write about the importance of the particular type of rock used to construct megalithic monuments, and the same principle may apply here: that the healing properties are inherent in the stone itself. As a battery will hold a charge of electricity, so certain stones of a specific granitic crystalline structure could have the property of storing the subtle health-giving energies, perhaps for centuries. When these stones are brought into contact with the life-field of the human body, or with a liquid, they are able to charge it with some of the stored energy. Perhaps some of these small stones were originally in the possession of a saint or a pre-Christian healer whose life-field has left a lasting impression on the stone, from which beneficial radiations can still be obtained by those in need. Alternatively, these small stones may be merely instruments to direct human mental powers. In the same way that a medium who concentrates on a crystal ball, or tea leaves in a cup, receives the ensuing revelations or predictions from her own subconscious via her psi abilities, not from the object she gazes into, the portable healing stones may have been used to help gather the patient's own mental healing powers which he then, unknowingly, focused on himself. His success depended on his having faith in the stone and believing in its ability to cure him. A modern analogy is the placebo or dummy medicine which is an accepted part of medical practice today. Patients who are given substances of no medicinal value but believe they are taking a powerful medicine sometimes obtain relief from their ailments.

Some stones may still retain their healing powers, and in support of this we quote from *Quicksilver Heritage*, where Paul Screeton tells of a stone at Hart (Cleveland) which has cured friends of his: 'One woman's rheumatism was so bad that she could not put her hands behind her head, but after sitting on the stone she found she was capable of doing this. Another man had injured an arm in a road accident, and several minutes after sitting on the stone the pain was 90 per cent gone.'

Fertility and childbirth

There are many traditions connecting stones with fertility and childbirth. Certain standing stones have been described as phallic symbols, though whether this was the original intention or is a Freudian interpretation from the twentieth century is not easy to decide. Sometimes phallus-shaped stones are found with diamond-shaped stones, which are said to represent the female principle, for example in the Avebury circle (Wiltshire), and also in the avenue of stones between Avebury and West Kennet. The female aspect could also be represented by the circle, as in holed stones like the Men-an-Tol (described earlier, under 'Healing stones'; the act of passing a sick child through the hole could symbolise rebirth), and, more generally, in stone circles. Sometimes these have female names and are accompanied by phallic standing stones with masculine-sounding names; for example, the Merry Maidens stone circle near Lamorna (Cornwall), close to which are the Pipers standing stones. If certain of the standing stones do have a phallic significance, perhaps it is not too far-fetched to imagine the earth currents flowing through them as the sacred semen, able to fertilise the land, crops, animals, and people if the correct rituals are performed.

On the Isle of Man there is a well that is associated with a monolith and both were considered efficacious in promoting the fertility of women. The stone is known as the White Lady of Ballafreer and the nearby well as

One of the diamond-shaped stones at Avebury.

Chibbyr Pherick, 'St Patrick's Well'. Here a girl who was soon to be married would fill her mouth with the well water and walk three times round the stone *jesh*-wise (sunwise), then swallow the potent water, saying 'Ayns yn Ennym Yee, as y Vac, as y Spyrryd Noo', which in the Manx tongue means, 'In the name of the Father and of the Son and of the Holy Ghost'. This must all be done before sunrise. The time of day is not specified in the next account, which comes from Salop. On that rocky ridge called the Wrekin there is a narrow cleft in the rocks known as the Needle's Eye. Traditionally every young woman who visited the area would scramble through the cleft and be met on the other side by her boy friend or fiancé, who would receive a kiss or, if this was not forthcoming, could demand a forfeit of any coloured ribbon or handkerchief that she might have with her. A girl who looked back while she was negotiating the cleft would never be married. Not very far away are the Stiperstones, and here too is another Needle's Eye which was negotiated by visitors.

There is a large erect stone named the Holed Stone a mile outside the village of Doagh (Antrim). It is about five feet tall and is perforated with a hole big enough to receive a person's hand. Here it has been the custom for local marriages to be ratified by the couple clasping hands through the hole. Large standing stones with a hole through them are often found to be

The Holed Stone at Doagh, where marriage contracts were ratified.

connected with marriage rites—another was the Woden Stone or Stone of Odin at Stenness, near Kirkwall, in Orkney. A couple who clasped hands through the hole and made a vow were considered to be married—a divorce could be obtained by both partners attending a church service and leaving by separate doors. This stone was destroyed in 1814. At Kil-chouslan, Kintyre (Strathclyde: Argyll), was a holed stone where tradi-tionally an eloping couple who clasped hands through the aperture were then safe from pursuit, and regarded as lawfully married. Further south, in the Isle of Man, a number of stone rings lie in the churchyard of Kirk Braddan. In past times these were used during a wedding ceremony, when the couple would clasp hands through the stones. Even further south, in the old abbey gardens of Tresco in the Scilly Isles, an upright stone has two holes through which engaged couples would pass their hands and then join them, plighting their troth.

These traditions all concern engagement and marriage. The next important event in most women's lives was childbirth, and to ensure that they did not remain childless they often resorted to those places where the fertilising influence of the earth currents could be absorbed. Many stones were credited with curing barrenness, but stones were also visited to ensure an easy birth; and the first story indicates that some women wished to waste no time in attaining the state of motherhood! At Warton in Lancashire a bride would go to the Bride's Chair, a seat-like depression on the crag, for to sit there on her wedding day would ensure fertility. Barren women went to sit upon a stone in Brahan Wood, three miles from Dingwall (Highland: Ross and Cromarty), so that they might become fertile; and King's Park, Edinburgh, had a large recumbent stone along which barren women slid in the hope that they would soon become mothers. In Grampian (Aberdeenshire), childless women were passed through a hole in the Kelpie Stane in the River Dee near Dinnet. Another stone where childless women came to receive the fertilising influence is Clach-na-Bhan (Stone of the Women), a granite mass on top of the hill Meall-Ghaineaih near Glenavon in Braemar (Grampian: Aberdeen). Near Arpafeelie, Black Isle (Highland: Ross and Cromarty), is a stone with a basin several inches deep formed in its surface. Women would visit it and wash in the water that collected within the hollow in order to cure barrenness.

A cuplike hollow in a memorial slab in the wall of Chapel Yard, a cemetery at Burghead (Grampian: Moray), is said to have been produced by children striking the slab with a beach stone. If they then quickly put their ears close to the slab, they claimed to hear the sound of a rocking cradle and a crying child, as if coming from deep underground—hence the name Cradle Stone given to the slab. This practice seems to be a fading memory of the slab's earlier fertility-producing attribute, because in the eighteenth century women who wished to become pregnant believed they

The Cradle Stone at Burghead was visited by women who wished to have children.

would do so if they heard a cradle and baby after tapping on the stone.

Belief in the fertilising qualities of certain stones has extended into the twentieth century, for as recently as 1923 women who went to London would clasp their arms round the pillars of St Paul's Cathedral in the hope that this would help them to conceive. A similar practice was found at Clonmacnoise (Offaly) where a man would span the shaft of the ancient cross near the ruined monastery with his arms; if he was able to bring his fingertips together whilst doing so, he could subsequently give relief to his wife, if she was experiencing painful childbirth, by placing his palms on her abdomen. The cross at Boho near Enniskillen (Fermanagh) was considered to have fertilising powers for men, though the practices they followed when visiting this site are not recorded.

A very recent case of fertilising power ascribed to stones comes from Paestum near Naples in Italy, where there is a temple built in 700 BC to a fertility goddess. In 1973 the Press carried a report that women from many countries were coming to this site in order to sit astride a three-foot stone, and there were those who said that after having done so they soon became pregnant.

Some stones were also thought to be efficacious in easing the process of childbirth. One practice that occurred at a number of sites was that of women pulling their clothing through a hole in a stone to ease the pangs of childbirth; this was done, for example, at the holed stone at Clocnapeacaib

Childless men visited this ornate cross at Boho in the hope of restoring their fertility.

in County Cork. On Aran Island, off the Irish coast, clothes were drawn through the five-foot holed stone at Mainister, but in this case by women who were sick. The Stone of the Women in Braemar, already mentioned as a source of fertilising power, was also used to ensure easy birth, and women who were about to give birth used to sit on it in the hope of a painless delivery. Similarly in the Isle of Man, the White Lady of Ballafreer, a quartz pillar also referred to earlier, was visited by pregnant women who performed the same ritual as that carried out by girls about to be married.

Fruitfulness and good fortune

The influences which flowed through the stones could not only bring wellbeing and fertility to the people, but also appear to have been able to cause the crops and cattle to flourish.

In the middle of the last century T. Quiller-Couch described a ceremony he witnessed at Respryn cross, St Winnow (Cornwall). He wrote, 'This Cross serves as a boundary mark, and it is the custom to visit it yearly, dig round it and throw some earth on its top.' The stone itself had a rough cross symbol carved on top, either a sun symbol or a later christianising cross, and it would seem very probable that the ceremony was all that remained of a fertilising act, bringing the earth into closer contact with emanations from the stone.

In Lincolnshire, at the village of Audeby, a local historian in the mid nineteenth century gathered from the local population a legend regarding the origin of Boundel's Stone, the large blue stone which stood near the centre of Boundel's Croft, an old enclosure in the village. It had, they said, been stolen from the Danes during the reign of King Lud, by one named Boundel. He took it during a time of famine, because of its magic powers: when it was beaten with hazel rods, rain fell. Boundel had a companion, Grim, on his adventure, and Grim stole another magic stone which, when beaten, made the corn grow, but then the Devil had flown away with Grim's stone. For a long while before this happened, however, everybody from the surrounding countryside attended an annual gathering and feast around the two stones, which were whipped 'till iverybody went wicked wi' prosperity'.

In Scotland, overlooking the Clyde Estuary near Gourock (Strathclyde: Renfrew), there is a block of stone seven feet high known as Granny Kempock, or the Kempock Stane. It was believed locally that Granny Kempock had powers over the seas and weather, and fishermen would bring gifts and baskets of sand from the shore. Whilst circling the stone several times they would sprinkle sand at its foot, asking for good weather, calm seas, and a large catch. Granny Kempock was also visited by newly married couples who would circle the stone holding hands and ask for a fruitful union. In 1662 Mary Lamont said that she had danced round the stone with the Devil, and they had planned to throw it into the sea to bring ill fortune to the fishing people and their boats. Mary Lamont and her friends were presumably witches, and an account of how the witches used Granny Kempock in order to influence the weather is given in Chapter Seven.

Another site in Scotland where ancient stones were thought to have influence over the weather is found in Glen Lyon (Tayside: Perth). There, in the stone hut called Tigh na Cailliche (the Hag's House), are three stones known as the Bodach (the Old Man), the Cailleach (the Hag), and the Nighean (the Daughter). During the winter months the stones are kept within the hut. Before each winter a local shepherd repairs the roof and walls of the hut to make sure the family is kept dry and sheltered throughout the winter. In the spring they are brought out into the sun and the hut is swept clean. These three stones are said to guarantee good pasturage and fine weather for the year. The local people have a story to explain the presence of the stones, which says that a man and his wife found shelter in the valley and the woman gave birth to a daughter. Later the three vowed to stay there for ever and protect the valley that had provided hospitality, and the stones commemorate these three. Undoubtedly this is another place where the fructifying forces were invoked, and the continued protection of the stones is all that remains of the ancient practices.

Mental influences

Not only were stones thought to be capable of affecting the physical condition of people; they were also considered to have an effect on their mental states too, and we find traditions which suggest that too close a proximity to some stones at certain times of the year could have a lasting effect upon a man's mental abilities. There is a cromlech in Dyffryn woods (probably Tinkinswood chambered cairn) near St Nicholas (South Glamorgan) where it was considered unlucky to sleep on the 'three spirit nights' of May Day eve, St John's eve (23 June), and Midwinter eve. Anyone ignoring this advice would be liable to die, go mad, or become a poet. The controlling spirits of this cromlech were thought to be those of the long-departed Druids, who would punish the wicked by beating them, and were particularly hard on drunkards. One such who spent a night at this site said that they 'beat him first, and then whirled him up to the sky, from which he looked down and saw the moon and stars thousands of miles below him. The Druids held him suspended by his hair in the mid-heaven, until the first peep of day, and then let him drop down to the Dyffryn woods, where he was found in a great oak by farm labourers', according to the account in *Folk-Lore and Folk-Stories of Wales* by Marie Trevelyan. It is interesting to note that this tale has echoes of some of the reported experiences of today's flying saucer contactees, who tell of flying around space and seeing the stars and the moon from the craft of the alien visitors. Close by, near St Lythans, the stones of St Lythans chambered cairn were said to grant a whispered wish on Hallowe'en. Whether the wish must be for good or ill is not known, but the field was unprofitable and the local people said the land was cursed.

The mountain of Cader Idris in Gwynedd (Merionethshire) has a strange reputation. Somewhere on its summit is the rock seat of the giant Idris, and here too, anyone who stays the night will find death or madness, or become a genius. On the first night of a new year mysterious lights are said to be seen near the peak, and again this sounds similar to today's reports of flying saucers or UFOs.

A famous figure from Wales's past, half fact, half legend, is the great bard Taliesin (one story of whose birth is given in Chapter Seven). Tradition places his grave in the parish of Llanfihangel Genau'r Glyn (Dyfed: Cardigan). The stone grave, known as Bedd Taliesin, is in the centre of a mound of earth surrounded by stone circles, and here too the tradition says that anyone who sleeps there for one night will become either a poet or an idiot.

In West Glamorgan, the underground dungeon at Oystermouth Castle, Gower, had a large pillar called the Wishing Post. Young men and women who desired to find a sweetheart would walk round this stone nine times while making their wish, and would 'stick a pin in the pillar'. Of the many wishing stones which were once probably to be found all over the British Isles, few are still known today. One such is the Wishing Stone among Brimham Rocks (near Ripley, North Yorkshire), where it was traditional to place the middle finger of one's right hand in the hole in the stone, and wish. At Matlock in Derbyshire the Lumsdale Wishing Stone is used by those who want their wishes granted, and believe that this will happen if they make a wish whilst standing on this flat outcrop of rock. It is also considered lucky to wish while standing on the eye of the white horse at Uffington (Oxfordshire). Torr mo Ghuidhe is Gaelic for Hillock of my Wish, a mound situated between Bonar Bridge and Altas on the old Sutherland/Ross and Cromarty border (Highland). A crofter living nearby earlier this century remembered that it had long been the custom to wish and to make compacts upon the mound. Further south, on the island of Islay (Strathclyde), there is in the churchyard of Kilchoman a Celtic cross standing on a square stone base. In each corner of the base is a hollow, and in one of these rests a marble ball. The belief now is that a turn of the ball will grant a wish, and as the hollow in which the ball rests is appreciably deeper than the others, it would seem that the ritual is often practised. The idea of small round stones being able to grant wishes seems to be a debased memory of the knowledge that they could in fact be made to hold an energy that was transmitted by the human mind, and presently we will examine some recent experiments that seem to strengthen this possibility.

In the remotest parts of Ireland and Scotland it was the practice until recent times (and who knows what practices may still be continued, unknown to the populace in general?) to resort to certain 'praying stones' at times of crisis. The island of Inishmurray in the Bay of Donegal (Sligo) has two standing stones, one on the southern side of the 'Church of the

Men', the other near the 'Church of the Women'. Both these monoliths have had a cross carved on them, but the most interesting feature is the holes cut in the edge of the stones, just large enough to take a finger. Before these two stones, men and women, and particularly women before childbirth, would kneel to pray, and it was generally considered that the holes had been cut to enable people to rise from the kneeling position with ease by placing their thumbs in the front holes and their forefingers in the side holes. Although this is the way they were used in recent years, it is not inconceivable that the original purpose was to make a positive contact between the hand and the stone, and that whilst the person was 'praying' or focusing his mental powers, the stones were clasped by using these holes and there was in this way a stronger interchange of energy between the stone and the person.

Another location, also in County Sligo, where close contact is made with stone is at Killery. In the graveyard of the old church is a thin flagstone on which lie seven egg-shaped stones. There is also a small piece of stone projecting from the soil, and this has a string round it. This 'straining string' is considered to be a certain cure for strains and aches and pains in general, and is removed by any who wish to use its curative powers. Anyone who does remove it must replace it with a similar string. The person seeking a cure then takes each of the seven stones in succession between the thumb and second finger of the left hand and turns it from left to right, at the same time repeating certain prayers—or might it be charms?

The egg-shaped stones, straining stone, and straining string at Killery.

Near the ruined church of Fernagh (Kerry) is a rock with eight 'cups' in its top surface, and a worn oval pebble lies in each depression. These are known as the Butter Rolls, and a story explains their presence. It tells how a local saint, to whom the church is dedicated, kept his cows nearby, but the woman who looked after them stole and sold the butter, and so the

M.F. WAKEMAN

The Clocha-breacha altar on the island of Inishmurray (Sligo) bears numerous cursing stones, said to be uncountable. It is only one of several such altars on the island. W. G. Wood-Martin shows that they still had a strong reputation at the time when he wrote *Traces of the Elder Faiths of Ireland*: 'In the year 1886, during the anti-Protestant riots in the town of Sligo, an aged countrywoman was heard to threaten that she would go to the Island and "turn the stones against the Protestants".'

saint turned her into stone, and the butter rolls into pebbles. Those who want to use the power of these stones turn them as they make their prayers.

Eriskay is one of the smaller islands in the southern part of the Western Isles, and here there is a standing stone eight feet high near the church of St Columba. This was one of the stones which were once carefully preserved by wrapping in flannel. It was known as a 'bowing stone', and the locals used to make their obeisances to it while reciting the Lord's Prayer (could this have replaced a pre-Christian ritual chant?). Stones of various sizes, often being kept wrapped in cloth and sometimes washed with water or milk, were treasured by families or clans. These stones were used as charms to obtain favourable winds, which were, of course, very important to the island fishing communities. Another stone used to influence the weather was kept on Fladda, a remote point of land north of Skye. It was a blue stone which lay on the altar of St Columba's chapel and was always kept moist. When the fishermen had unfavourable winds they washed the stone with the expectation of changing the wind to a favourable one. This stone was also used as an 'oath stone' and a 'curing stone'. The difference between oath stones, healing stones, cursing stones, stones to influence the weather, and so on, was probably no more than the use to which they were put. As with all forms of magical manipulation, the energy invoked is the same. Whether the intention is for good or evil is the determining factor.

Similar stones to the rock at Fernagh with its eight 'cups', mentioned above, are found elsewhere in Ireland, and there are a number of 'altars' built of stone blocks which have groups of rounded water-worn stones placed on top of them. These are often termed cursing stones. To turn the cursing stones of Kilmoon (Clare) will cause the victim's mouth to twist awry, and there is an altar for cursing in the graveyard at Killeany (also in County Clare). On the island of Iniskill, near Port Noo (Donegal), is a small boulder of dark slate about eighteen inches long, with four bands of quartz running through it. It is long and egg-shaped, pointed at the ends, and, if natural, was probably rolled into this shape by the sea. It rests with other stones on top of a square natural block, and during the summer was an object of pilgrimage. The pilgrims passed the stone around amongst themselves while repeating prayers or curses. Cromarty (Highland: Ross and Cromarty) had its Stone of Cursing, a big boulder known locally as Clach na Mullachd. To deliver a curse a man would stand or kneel on it with bare knees (i.e. in uninterrupted contact with the stone). There was a cursing well at St Elian, near Colwyn Bay (Clwyd: Denbigh), where stones marked with the initials of the victims were dropped into the water.

In County Sligo both Ballysummaghan and Barroe had stones that were used for cursing; but the person placing the curse had to be bareheaded and barefoot while doing so. To avert the curse, the person against whom the stones were turned was ritually buried in a grave dug for the purpose, by having three shovelsful of earth scattered on him while those above recited the appropriate rhymes or charms. Burying alive (except for the head) was often used to ward off ill luck or as a cure for insanity. The original intention behind this practice could have been to bring the sufferer into the most intimate contact with the healing earth currents and thereby restore a balance to his physical and mental structure; or alternatively, to 'earth' the body and thereby drain off the malignant energy with which it had been charged. A report in the *Leicester and Nottingham Journal* for 13 May 1775 shows that the same cure was used for physical as well as mental ailments. Unfortunately the report does not mention the actual location of the experiment, though presumably it was in Leicestershire or Nottinghamshire.

Churchyard Mould a cure for Rheumatism—This day a very odd experiment was tried upon a young man about twenty-five years of age, who was much afflicted with the rheumatism. He was ordered to be buried in the earth for two hours, naked, his face only uncovered; which operation was accordingly performed, and he lay the time. The man says he feels himself much better; it is said he is to be buried again to-morrow for three hours.

The island of Inishmurray in Donegal Bay is especially noteworthy for its stone altars topped with cursing stones. These stones are all of a regular rounded shape and are often considered to be of natural waterworn origin, though we do not know that this has been proved to be the case. They can vary in size from an inch or so in diameter up to two feet or more across, though the usual size seems to be about four to eight inches. Some of these stones have designs inscribed upon them, often a variation of the cross, and they have a strong similarity to the psychotronic generators made and used by Robert Pavlita and described in *Psychic Discoveries Behind the Iron Curtain* (Ostrander and Schroeder). This Czech inventor has made a

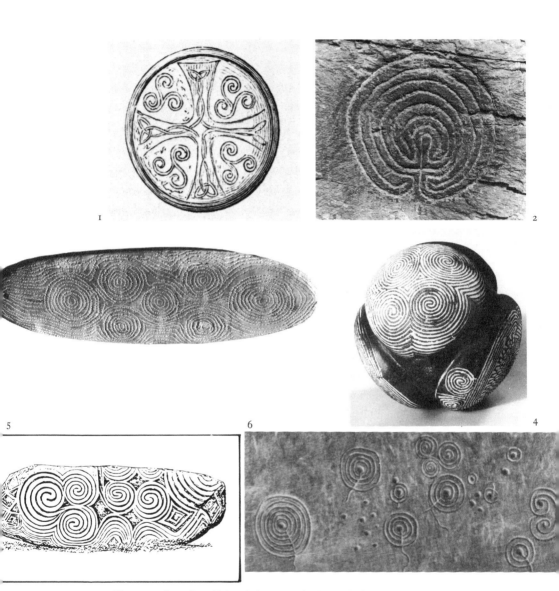

Six examples of traditional designs which might have been used in the manner of 'staring patterns' as described in the text. (1) Cursing stone from the island of Inishmurray (Sligo); (2) Labyrinth of unknown date carved on rock at Rocky Valley near Tintagel (Cornwall); (3) Australian aborigine tjuringa used for divination purposes; (4) A stone ball discovered at Towie (Grampian) in 1860, with three faces intricately patterned. The ball has been chalked so that the designs stand out clearly; (5) Carving on the entrance stone at Newgrange passage grave (Meath); (6) An example of the cup and ring marks found carved on rocks in many parts of the British Isles, especially northern England and Scotland.

number of these generators of various metals and inscribed with lines or 'staring patterns'. By moving his eyes along the lines and following the pattern, a person using one of these 'generators' will cause it to be charged with an energy that is largely unknown to science. A few scientists, principally in eastern Europe, are now researching into this hitherto little-known force, which is variously termed 'psychotronic' by the Czechs, 'bioplasmic' by the Soviets, or 'psychic' in the West, and is probably the 'vital energy' known to the ancient Chinese and referred to as 'prana' in old Hindu texts. Pavlita's generators are inscribed with a zigzag pattern similar to a figure eight, which is also a good description of the design within the cross motif in the illustration of the cursing stone from Inishmurray.

In 1860 at Towie (Grampian: Aberdeen), a stone ball was discovered that was covered in double spirals and other complex patterns, again somewhat reminiscent of the psychic generators and cursing stones. Other strange carved stones, globe- or drum-shaped, have been found at various sites in Britain, and have remained one of the mysteries of archaeology, but these artefacts could well be earlier forms of cursing stones or psychic generators. This idea could also be extended to include such enigmas as cup and ring marks and other prehistoric rock carvings. Pavlita has found that his generators can release their energy and cause small wheels to turn, or are able to charge a rod which can then be used to pick up non-ferrous metals and minerals. They have also been used to increase plant growth and slightly alter the molecular structure of water. Another Czech, Dr Zdenek Rejdak, is reported to have used one of these generators in telepathy experiments. Using a conventional pack of twenty-five Zener cards bearing five symbols, he found that a sender who turned up a card from the pack could influence the generator, several rooms away, to swing with its pointer to the same symbol on the display in front of it, thus establishing that energy can flow from the human mind into the generator.

Such experiments, and others being conducted today, indicate the feasibility of a belief in the ability of one mind to influence another at a distance. If we relate this knowledge to the cursing stones, it seems possible that wishes, prayers, and curses were able to be placed into stones and the beneficent or maleficent energy released later to have its effect upon the intended recipient. Alternatively, the effect of concentrating on the 'staring pattern' on the cursing stone, bringing the full force of the sender's malice into play, could have resulted in the malice being transmitted telepathically and instantaneously to the unfortunate recipient. If we extend this idea and suggest that cup and ring marks and other prehistoric rock carvings were also intended to work as 'staring patterns', perhaps they could have been used to help produce or distribute the earth current, by concentration as already described. The widespread distribution of such enigmatic

The Coronation Stone at Kingston-upon-Thames formerly stood inside the Saxon chapel of St Mary, until that building collapsed in 1730, since when it has had several outdoor locations. It was moved to its present site in 1936.

carvings throughout the British Isles, as described by Evan Hadingham in his *Ancient Carvings in Britain*, gives strength to this possibility.

Inauguration stones

Celtic and Saxon kings were once installed standing or sitting upon a sacred stone used only for this purpose, and it seems possible that they absorbed energy from the stone during the ceremony. Perhaps the inauguration stone most widely known today is that which now rests beneath the Coronation Chair in Westminster Abbey, London. This Stone of Destiny was brought from Scone in Scotland by order of Edward I in 1297 and placed beneath the wooden throne which had been made specially for it. Thirty-four successive kings of Scotland had been crowned sitting over it, and since it was brought to London in the thirteenth century every British monarch, except the first Mary, has sat above it during the inauguration ceremony of the coronation.

The Coronation Stone of the Royal Borough of Kingston-upon-Thames (Greater London) can still be seen set outdoors near the Guildhall in that ancient town. Upon this stone sat seven Saxon kings who were crowned during the tenth century, but nothing seems to be known of its earlier history. The small remnant of another stone of great antiquity can be seen in London, in a niche in the wall of the Bank of China in Cannon Street. This, the London Stone, was originally a large stone set well into the ground, across which the citizens made their pacts and from which they issued proclamations. That it had a tradition of conferring authority is shown by the action of the rebel Jack Cade when he entered the city in 1450. He struck the stone with his sword and announced, 'Now is Mortimer [i.e. himself] lord of this city', the significance of this symbolic action doubtless being understood by his fellows. A stone of seemingly similar importance was known in Devon at Bovey Tracey. This was in the form of a cross, and on Mayor's Day the Mayor struck it with his stick and the young men of the parish would kiss the stone and swear to uphold ancient rights and privileges. Also in Devon is the Brutus Stone at Totnes, upon which the Mayor stands to announce the accession of a monarch. It is supposed to mark the spot where Brutus landed in Britain, but its name is more likely to be derived from the name Bruiter's Stone, a stone used for proclamations by the town-crier (from the French *bruire*, to sound).

The Black Stone of Iona (Strathclyde) was kept in the cathedral, but it was lost in 1830. It was upon this stone that the Highland chiefs made their binding contracts and took solemn oaths. On Islay (Strathclyde) there was a Stone of Inauguration or Stone of the Footmarks by Loch Finlaggan. It was seven feet square and had footprints cut into it. When a chief of Clan Donald was installed as 'King of the Isles' he stood barefoot on the imprints

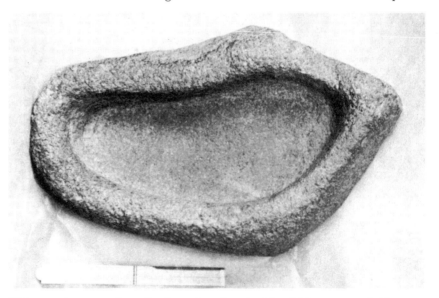

This swearing stone from Castleward earthwork, Isle of Man, was probably used in the same way as the stones bearing footprints which are described in the text.

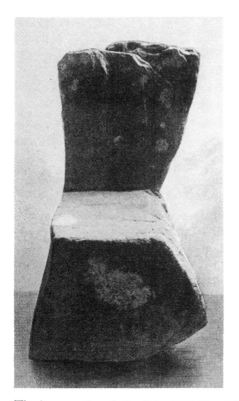

The inauguration chair of the O'Neills of Castlereagh.

on the stone, and with his father's sword in his hand was anointed king by the Bishop of Argyll and seven priests. During the ceremony an orator recited a catalogue of his ancestors, and he was proclaimed 'Macdonald, high prince of the Seed of Conn'. But nothing now remains of this ancient block, for it was deliberately destroyed in the early seventeenth century.

In Ireland the O'Neills of Castlereagh near Belfast were inaugurated upon a chairlike block of undressed whinstone. In the reign of James I the family met with misfortune and the chair was overturned. In 1750 it was moved to the Butter Market and was rescued from destruction by a gentleman who used it as a garden seat. Further south in the Loughcrew Hills (Westmeath) is the Hag's Chair, ten feet long, six feet high, and two feet thick, and weighing about ten tons. The centre is hollowed out in the rough form of a seat with each end raised about nine inches. That the seat was of interest to men in ancient times is shown by the concentric circles and zigzag carvings on its surface, and it has been tentatively identified by one person as the seat of Ollamh Fodhla, a king and lawmaker of prehistory.

There was at one time at Templemore in County Londonderry a slab that was latterly named St Columbkille's Stone, which had the imprints of two feet, each ten inches in length, upon its top surface. Traditionally it was one of the inauguration stones of the ancient Irish chieftains, and would doubtless have been used in a similar way to the footprinted stone on Islay, already described. The most famous inauguration stone in Ireland, upon which the kings of that country were installed, was known as the Lia Fail and was situated at Tara in County Meath. This magical stone could unfailingly identify the true king, and it emitted a shriek or roar that could be heard for many miles when he stood upon it. The present Coronation Stone in Westminster Abbey, London, is usually identified as the Lia Fail, but Lewis Spence in *The Magic Arts in Celtic Britain* states that the Lia Fail is still in Ireland at Tara and is known to the Irish anti-quarians. It does not resemble the Coronation Stone, being a pillar and not easily transported.

The feature common to these stones of inauguration is that the initiate either sat upon them or made close contact with bare hands or bare feet. This could enable the earth currents to flow through the body and thus 'charge' the recipient with the requisite energies and vitality to enable him to exercise his powers as a representative of the gods upon earth.

3 'A strange and monstrous serpent...'

Although they are not always directly associated with ancient sites, dragons (also known as serpents and worms) and their activities are highly relevant to any study of the earth currents. It is often assumed that Britain's sole link with these fabulous beasts is through the dragon-killing exploits of England's patron saint St George, but there is a vast, largely unconsidered, lore concerning dragons, and stories about them have been current for hundreds of years in all areas of the British Isles. What are we to make of such stories? There are several possible interpretations. Dragons may have been: (1) A fiction, pure and simple; (2) Allegories, symbols of something else; (3) Real live creatures, a species of gigantic saurian now extinct but still remembered through countless generations; (4) More mundane creatures unintentionally misrepresented; (5) A memory of Danish invasions (their standards showed a dragon); (6) Unidentified flying objects; (7) Psychic apparitions. Any one of these possibilities, or several of them together, could explain dragon encounters, depending on the circumstances of each individual case. Here we will describe some of the more complex dragon stories, concentrating especially on those which have connections with ancient sites, and also on those which might help to clarify or extend our knowledge of the workings of the earth current.

Dragons at large

In a number of tales, the dragons are just described matter-of-factly, as though they are an accepted part of the fauna of a district, with little or no attempt being made to exterminate them, even though they do sometimes feast upon cattle and people. Some of the stories are surprisingly recent, such as the account of the dragon of St Leonard's Forest (West Sussex), which is dated 1614. The validity of such 'modern' tales is doubted by many, and it has been suggested that the St Leonard's Forest dragon was a serpent or tropical lizard escaped from a private menagerie. This theory has frequently been offered as an explanation when an unusual animal starts to make intermittent appearances in a district. The most noted case in recent years is that of the 'Surrey puma', though it has been seen in places far distant from Surrey—and even in two widely separated places at the same time! It is most unlikely that pumas are escaping from private zoos all over the south of England; and it is equally unlikely that a serpent or lizard answering the description of the St Leonard's Forest dragon likewise escaped in 1614, not to mention all the other 'dragons' that have been reported over the centuries.

A pamphlet describing the St Leonard's Forest dragon was headed: 'A True and Wonderful Discourse relating a strange and monstrous Serpent (or Dragon) lately discovered, and yet living, to the great Annoyance and

St Leonard's Forest is quiet today, but is supposed once to have been the haunt of a fearsome dragon.

divers Slaughters of both Men and Cattell, by his strong and violent Poison: in Sussex, two Miles from Horsam, in a Woode called St Leonard's Forrest, and thirtie Miles from London, this present Month of August, 1614. With the true Generation of Serpents.' In this pamphlet, the creature is described as

nine feete, or rather more, in length, and shaped almost in the forme of an axle-tree of a cart; a quantitie of thickness in the middest, and somewhat smaller at both endes. The former part, which he shootes forth as a necke, is supposed to be

This dragon with a toothy grin, illustrated in Topsell's *Historie of Foure-Footed Beastes* (1607), is not a real dragon at all, but goes by the name of Jenny Haniver, which is a name used by antiquarians to describe man-made fabulous beasts. In the sixteenth and seventeenth centuries, there was a steady manufacture of non-existent creatures from parts taken from animals, fishes, and birds, some of them most skilfully done.

an elle long; with a white ring, as it were, of scales about it. The scales along his backe seem to be blackish, and so much as is discovered under his bellie, appeareth to be red; . . . It is likewise discovered to have large feete, but the eye may be there deceived; for some suppose that serpents have no feete . . . [He] rids away (as we call it) as fast as a man can run. He is of countenance very proud, and at the sight or hearing of men or cattel, will raise his neck upright, and seem to listen and looke about, with great arrogancy. There are likewise upon either side of him discovered, two great bunches so big as a large foote-ball, and (as some thinke) will in time grow to wings; but God, I hope, will (to defend the poor people in the neighbourhood) that he shall be destroyed before he grow so fledge.

The dragon was thought to live on rabbits; although he (or rather the 'venome' he shot forth) killed dogs and people, he did not eat them. It is also interesting that always 'in his track or path [he] left a glutinous and slimie matter . . . which is very corrupt and offensive to the scent . . .'

Dragons or winged serpents were also a familiar sight in the woods around Penllyne Castle (South Glamorgan) in earlier days, according to nineteenth-century folklore. One old man remembered hearing in his boyhood that the winged serpents were very beautiful. They rested coiled up, and looked as if covered with jewels; some had sparkling crests. If disturbed, they glided to their hiding-places with outspread wings. They became extinct because they took poultry, and people killed them for it. An old woman related her memories of the winged serpents in Penmark Place (South Glamorgan), and they too were as notorious as foxes in the farmyards. Her grandfather had tried to kill one in the woods of Porthkerry Park; he and his companion were attacked when they wounded a winged serpent with gunshot, but after a fierce fight they killed it. She had seen its skin and feathers. Winged serpents were not peculiar to south Wales, stories about them being current in all the wilder parts of that country—Penmaenmawr, the Berwyns, Cader Idris, Plinlimmon, Radnor Forest, and Brecon Beacons.

Not all dragons were native, it seems, nor were they peculiar to Britain. Four hundred years after the event it is difficult to determine the identity of a 'monstrous serpent' brought to Durham from Ethiopia. The quotation comes from St Nicholas's Register, Durham.

1568, Mdm. that a certain Italian brought into the citie of Durham, the 11th day of June, in the yeare above sayd, a very great strange and monstrous serpent, in length sixteen feet, in quantitie and dimensions greater than a great horse; which was taken and killed by speciall pollicie in Æthiopia, within the Turkes dominions. But before it was killed, it had devoured (as is credibly thought) more than 1000 persons, and destroyed a whole countrey.

These are just a sample of dragon traditions, showing that their presence was widespread and, sometimes, well documented.

Water monsters

One aspect of the dragon tradition which is as strong now, in the 1970s, as it ever was is the reported appearance of those dragons which seem to prefer (or to need) to live in a body of water. What physical relationship water monsters have to dragons and winged serpents is difficult to decide, for in all categories the descriptions of the creatures often vary considerably, but that there is a relationship of some kind cannot be doubted. A more precise study of their physical characteristics than there is room for here might come up with some illuminating results. Water monsters, both factual and traditional, have been carefully studied and much written about, but, so far as we are aware, land-dragons/serpents/worms have not. F. W. Holiday, who has developed some unusual theories on dragons, comments in his book *The Dragon and the Disc*: 'All Peistes [water-horses], Worms, Serpents, and Dragons share a common feature—they came out of water.' He then gives a number of examples of land dragons which originally emerged from rivers, streams or marshes. However, that they were all the same species is by no means certain; those we call water monsters, such as the Loch Ness monster, have been seen out of the water, but apparently spend most of their time in it; the land dragons, on the other hand, while possibly originating in water, live for the most part out of it; and thirdly the *winged* serpents would seem to be yet another species. But such discussions, though diverting, are irrelevant, and so for our present purposes we have grouped all dragons, serpents, worms, etc., together.

One of several photographs of the Loch Ness monster, this picture was taken in 1955. The building on the right is the ruined Urquhart Castle.

The best-known modern dragon has been for many years the Loch Ness monster (or monsters), said to inhabit that deep and eerie body of water in the Highlands of Scotland. Despite numerous sightings both in and out of water, and scientific expeditions manned specifically to solve the mystery, the monster has evaded capture with apparent ease, and only provided a few enigmatic sonar and photographic records for scientists to examine. This leads the sceptical to doubt its existence, but can we dismiss the many reports received from convinced (not necessarily beforehand, but certainly afterwards) eye-witnesses? Other lakes in Scotland, Wales, and Ireland also claim their water monsters, and some books are listed in the bibliography for those who wish to read more on this subject.

Water-loving dragons were/are not only to be found in large mountain lakes, however. The 'Knucker' lived in the Knucker Hole, a deep pool near Lyminster church (West Sussex)*; and winged serpents sometimes

* *Nicor* is the Saxon word for 'sea monster', so this tradition would seem to go back at least to Saxon times.

curled up in wells, for example Grinston Well in Brawdy parish (Dyfed: Pembroke), the Well of the Maidens (Grampian: Aberdeen), and the Serpent Well (Ffynon Sarff) in Llanengan parish (Gwynedd: Caernarvon). Perhaps in such traditions as these the serpent symbolises the healing 'serpent' power or potency contained within the well.

Dragon or UFO?

Some 'dragons' may not have been living creatures at all. Dragons were part of the folklore of the Middle Ages, therefore any large, strange flying creature or object was likely to be called a dragon. Flying craft were unthought of then, of course. But the so-called dragons may sometimes have been what are now termed 'flying saucers', or, to give them their current scientific title, 'UFOs'—unidentified flying objects. These have been seen throughout the centuries, and all over the world, being described according to the familiar terminology of the time. In the martial civilisation of the Romans, for example, such an inexplicable sight was described as a 'flying shield'. Readers of UFO literature will be familiar with the incredibly varied descriptions of the craft which have been seen, and will realise that the phenomena are often too extraordinary for the witnesses to describe, let alone comprehend, so that the suggested parallel between the reaction of the present-day UFO witness and that of the dragon-spotter of yesteryear is a valid one.

The behaviour of a 'dragon' which manifested itself in Suffolk in the early fifteenth century has certain similarities to the activities of UFOs in our present century. This description, dating from 1405, is by a monk, John de Hokelowe.

Close to the town of Bures, near Sudbury, there has lately appeared, to the great hurt of the countryside, a Dragon, vast in body with a crested head, teeth like a saw, and a tail extending to enormous length. Having slain the shepherd of a flock, he then devoured many sheep. There came forth in order to shoot at him with arrows the workmen of the lord on whose domain he had concealed himself, being Sir Richard de Waldegrave, knight; but the Dragon's body, although struck by archers, remained unhurt, for the arrows bounced off his back as if it were iron or hard rock. Those arrows that fell upon the spine of his back gave out as they struck a ringing or tinkling sound, just as if they had hit a brazen plate and then flew far away off by reason of the hide of this great beast being impenetrable. Thereupon, in order to destroy him, all the country people around were summoned. But when the Dragon saw that he was again about to be assailed by arrows, he fled into a marsh or mere and there hid himself amongst the long reeds; nor was he any more seen.

Three outstanding similarities between dragons and UFO activity are demonstrated here:

1. This dragon devoured sheep: UFOs have been known to abduct cattle, especially in the United States (but for what purpose is not known).
2. Arrows 'bounced off his back as if it were iron or hard rock': as they naturally would do if the object were of artificial construction rather than a living creature. In recent years, bullets fired at UFOs have similarly ricocheted off the impervious 'skin'.
3. The dragon 'fled into a marsh or mere': in other words, the UFO absented itself; to where, the people knew not. UFOs are known for their apparently erratic behaviour, and their sudden disappearances, which, it has been suggested, are actually dematerialisations. 'Nor was he any more seen' could indeed be true, if the UFO dematerialised among the reeds. It would be strange if a large dragon were not seen any more, with no corpse having come to light to show that it had died or been killed.

Crowcombe church (Somerset) has a fine set of early sixteenth-century carved bench-ends, one of which depicts two men despatching a terrifying monster. At the bottom left is another head with a vine issuing from its mouth. This was possibly a symbolic reference to the fertilising influence of the 'dragon lines' or earth currents.

It is true that the description of the 'dragon' does not by any stretch of the imagination resemble that of a UFO—at least, that is, the UFOs seen in this century. Who knows what the UFOs of several centuries ago looked like! They have appeared in many guises recently, from airships at the turn of the century to smooth, streamlined space-craft, and if they are phantoms rather than solid objects, then the traditional dragon disguise need not be so very unlikely: 'crested head, teeth like a saw, and a tail extending to enormous length'. On the other hand, this description could simply have been a rationalisation of the unknown, the features described being a very liberal interpretation of the UFO's external appearance. It is unlikely that anyone ventured too near the strange visitor, and so all who saw it gained only an overall impression, which was anyway probably influenced by excitement and fear. In our own times, it is frequently reported how notoriously inaccurate are people's powers of observation, as demonstrated when several eye-witness reports of a traffic accident are compared.

Another so-called dragon which may have been a UFO was briefly and tantalisingly reported in the *Baker's Chronicle*: 'In the seventeenth year of Henry the Second, AD 1170, there was seen at St. Osythes [Essex] a dragon of marvellous bigness, which, by moving, burned houses.' The 'fiery serpent' of Newcastle Emlyn (Dyfed: Carmarthen) may also have been a UFO. This strange visitation happened, according to some accounts, as late as the eighteenth century. Out of the blue, a *gwiber* or dragon was seen to alight on top of the ruined castle, and the many people attending a fair in the town were terrified. The creature was described as having a hard and stony substance or shell covering its whole body, except the navel, and a soldier who volunteered to kill the dragon aimed with his gun at this vulnerable point. He had prepared for his escape from the maddened creature by placing a piece of red flannel as a decoy on the surface of the river in which he was standing to fire at his target. As expected, the serpent attacked the red flannel and the soldier swam to safety. Soon the water was coloured with the blood of the dragon, for the shot had mortally wounded it.

It may be suggested that what the drink-befuddled merrymakers actually saw was a large bird, such as an eagle, perched on the castle, but their eyesight cannot have been so bad for we have the precise description of the 'hard and stony substance or shell covering its whole body', which does not sound like feathers. However, if this was no dragon, or eagle, but a UFO, this 'shell' could have been the material of which the UFO was constructed, and the so-called 'navel' might have been some clear marking on the underside of the UFO in a place corresponding to the navel on a living creature. (One could at this point get even more involved by remarking that only mammals have navels, whereas serpents and lizards are not mammals but egg-laying creatures, so *if* it were true that a dragon was seen at Newcastle Emlyn, and *if* it were true that it had a navel, this would surely shed some light on the biological nature of the creature called winged serpent or dragon!) The UFO explanation falls down at the point when the creature/craft attacked the piece of red flannel and its blood was seen to mingle with the river water. There is no obvious way of interpreting this part of the sighting if the *gwiber* was not a living creature.

Dragons and ancient sites

A possible significance of some of the dragon stories begins to emerge when we study the tales of dragons which are directly concerned with ancient sites. The dragon is usually imagined to be a powerful beast, fearful to behold, with poisonous breath; as an 'unknown factor' only to be tackled by a brave and cunning hero. These are characteristics which could also be attributable to the earth current, the forceful energy residing in the stones, mounds, and sacred places. There are indications in some of the dragon stories that these attributes do relate to the earth current. In Avon are two hillforts, Cadbury Camp and Dolebury Hill (near Clevedon), and a dragon was said to fly between them. Perhaps this is another way of saying that they are connected by a ley. There is a tradition that treasure was buried at both sites, this belief being perpetuated in the rhyme:

> If Cadbury and Dolebury dolven were
> All England might plough with a golden share.

As suggested in Chapter One, buried treasure might symbolise the earth current. Strangely, a Cadbury Camp and a Dolebury Hill are close together in south Devon, and the same tradition and rhyme apply. An occurrence noted in D. A. Mac Manus's fascinating book *The Middle Kingdom* might be relevant here, though no dragon is mentioned. Two 'fairy forts' in Ireland, one called Crillaun (Mayo), are the location of the occurrence, which was in fact one of several similar happenings. On this particular occasion, one Hallowe'en evening, the witness saw Crillaun fort lit up with hundreds of little white lights. She watched as they all rose into the air, and flew in a straight line across the loch to the other fort. Could an occurrence such as this have given rise to the 'flying dragon' story told about Cadbury Camp and Dolebury Hill? What the lights were is difficult to decide, but it is not outside the bounds of possibility that they had some connection with the earth current and were following the course of a ley from one fort to the other.

Several other traditions connect dragons with buried treasure. For example, an earthwork called Money Hill on Gunnarton Fell, Halliburn

(Northumberland) was said to have a dragon-guarded hoard of treasure; Castle Neroche in Somerset (a motte and bailey near Ilminster) was the haunt of a dragon who was a treasure guardian; and a hoard of gold in a barrow at Wormelow (worm = dragon, low = mound) in Salop was protected by a dragon.

Dragons were often slain by human heroes, if the old tales are to be believed, but sometimes they fought each other. Two dragons slept in a lake beneath the hill on which the hillfort of Dinas Emrys (near Nant Gwynant, Gwynedd: Caernarvon) was eventually built, and when the lake was drained, the dragons began to fight. One was white, representing the Saxons, and the other was red, representing Wales. The red dragon was victorious, and so became the emblem of Wales. A similar battle took place on the Suffolk-Essex border on the afternoon of Friday, 26 September 1449 (the precision of this dating is surprising), according to a contemporary chronicle which is now in Canterbury Cathedral. The site of the conflict was a marshy field known as Sharpfight Meadow, near Little Cornard, and a red and spotted dragon from Ballington Hill, Essex, defeated a black dragon from Kedington Hill, Suffolk. Although such stories are not literally true, they are important because of what they symbolise. If 'dragons' and the 'earth current' are synonymous, then a fight between two dragons might symbolise some natural event like an earth tremor, or a disaster caused by misuse of the earth current. In Chapter Eight we cite some examples of apparently natural catastrophes possibly caused by tampering with the earth currents.

Dragons slain

> 'Murder! murder! the Dragon cryed,
> Alack! alack! for grief;
> Had you but miss't that place you would
> Have done me no mischief.
> Then his head he shak't,
> Trembled and quaik't,
> And down he layed, and cried;
> First on one knee,
> Then on back tumbled he,
> So groaned, kick't, burst, and dyed.'*

Finally we come to the largest category of dragon lore, that involving the killing of dragons, serpents, or worms which are preying on the countryside,

---

* The last verse of the nineteen comprising 'A True Relation of the Dreadful Combate Between More of More Hall and the Dragon of Wantley' (or Wortley, near Rotherham, South Yorkshire), a broadside ballad issued in 1685.

killing cattle, and sometimes even people. There are many tales of these heroic deeds—we have details of over thirty, and there are probably many more as yet undiscovered in little-known writings or even forgotten because they have never been permanently recorded—but we will mention only a few because they tend to be repetitive, in that the emphasis is on the details of the killing, and despite their interest are not of great importance in our enquiry.

As far as is known of the facts of his life, St George neither visited England nor killed a dragon, but that mythical exploit has become firmly attached to his name, and the actual site has even been identified—as Dragon Hill, near Uffington (Oxfordshire), a truncated cone beneath the eye of the Uffington white horse (or dragon) where a patch of grassless soil marks the spot where the dragon's blood fell; or alternatively, as a field called Lower Stanks north of Brinsop church (Hereford and Worcester). South of the church is Dragon's Well, and inside the church itself is an eleventh-century tympanum showing St George in action. Author and antiquarian Harold Bayley, who revelled in discovering the basic meaning behind words, has made an interesting point concerning 'George' in his *The Lost Language of Symbolism*. He says: '*Ge*, as in *geography*, meant *earth*, so that the true meaning of *George* may legitimately be surmised as *Ge urge*, the urger or stimulator of the Earth.' Here is St George's role: to regulate the powerful earth currents, symbolised by the dragon.

Overleaf: Dragon Hill near Uffington, with the eye of the white horse in the foreground.

Twelfth-century tympanum in Brinsop church, showing St George killing the dragon. In this and similar cases, did the carving come first, with the local dragon-slaying tradition arising as a result? Or was the carving done to perpetuate an older tradition or body of knowledge?

The old dragon-slaying tales tell us that dragons frequently coiled themselves round hills that were convenient to their lairs. During the day the notorious Lambton Worm of Durham coiled himself round a rock in the River Wear, and by night he twined round Worm Hill near Fatfield. Nine times round he stretched, at his largest, which makes him about two miles long, according to one folklorist. Another says three times rather than nine, but perhaps that was when he was younger, and had not drunk so much milk (he grew accustomed to drink the milk of nine cows every day). The dragon of Linton (Borders: Roxburgh) had a den in Linton Hill, but occasionally he emerged and coiled around a hill by the name of Wormington or Wormistonne. According to one version, in *Folk Lore of the Northern Counties of England and the Borders* by William Henderson, 'while dying, the [Linton] worm is said to have contracted its folds with such violent muscular energy, that the sides of Wormington Hill are still marked with their spiral impressions'. The dragon of Bignor Hill in West Sussex used to coil himself round the hill, and the marks can still be seen. Explained quite simply, natural or man-made marks on a hill may have given rise to the belief that they were caused by a dragon. Or if we reject this as being an underestimation of the intelligence of our rural ancestors and go instead for a more symbolic interpretation, it may be that the hills concerned are not wholly natural but are part of the 'power circuit', a fact remembered unconsciously down the ages and brought to the surface by an association with that symbol of the terrestrial current, the dragon.

Some dragon killings are linked with ancient sites, for example La Hougue Bie, a burial mound near Five Oaks in Jersey (Channel Islands), where a dragon was killed by the Seigneur de Hanbye. Two mounds actually mark the burial places of slain dragons—the Bedd yr Afanc (Avanc's Grave) near Brynberian (Dyfed: Pembroke), where a dangerous monster was buried after being caught in a pool in the river, and Dun Dreggan (the dun of the great beast or dragon) in Glenmoriston (Highland:

Linton Hill, haunt of the Linton worm, seen from Linton church where there is an old and weatherworn carved tympanum above the door said to depict the slaying of the dragon by John Somerville. Known as the Somerville Stone, the tympanum came from the church which stood on the site (a prominent knoll of sand, different from the surrounding soil) before the present, relatively modern, church.

Inverness), where a dragon was slain by Fionn and his men after a great battle. Fionn built a dun (a fort or fortified dwelling place) beside the dragon's grave and it eventually became a haunt of the Little People.

Dragons were sometimes killed near old stones, which are probably ancient standing stones. The Sockburn worm was killed beside a stone, the Graystane, in a field near the church at Sockburn (Durham), as described in this quotation from the Bowes Manuscripts: 'Sir John Connyers, knight, slew that monstrous and poysonous vermine or wyverne, and aske or werme, which overthrew and devoured many people in fight, for that the sent of that poison was so strong that no person might abyde it, and by the providence of Almighty God this John Connyers, knight, overthrew the saide monster and slew it.'

Martin's Stone, Kirkton of Strathmartine (Tayside: Angus) is a three-foot boulder marking the spot where a dragon was slain by one Martin. However the fact that it is a Pictish standing stone with carvings of strange creatures suggests that the carvings gave rise to the dragon story. (Though Henry Bett, when giving more details of the involved story in his book *English Legends*, suggests it arose out of the nearby place name Baldragon.)

The story of the dragon of Ludham in Norfolk is an intriguing one. This scourge of the village had a lair to which he returned every morning after his nightly escapades, and the villagers often blocked up the entrance with bricks and stones. This proved useless, however, until one afternoon the dragon emerged to bask in the sunshine. Someone placed a single round stone in the lair entrance which blocked it completely, and the dragon was furious when he found he could not move the stone. He went angrily across the fields towards the Bishop's Palace, along a causeway and under an arch to the ruined St Benet's Abbey, and there he disappeared in the subterranean vaults, never to reappear. His route, taking in two old sacred sites, an ancient causeway, and an old archway (remember that abbeys and old stretches of road are often to be found on leys), could have been along a line of current. Close by is Cold Harbour Farm, and it has been noted by Watkins and others how often 'cole' or 'cold' and variations on them appear in close connection with leys. The route of the Mordiford dragon (Hereford and Worcester), who used to go down a track called Serpent's Lane to drink at the spot where the River Lugg joins the River Wye, could also have been a ley; and doubtless careful search would reveal many more links of a similar kind.

Frequent mention is made of the dragon's poisonous breath or venom. The slayer of the Linton worm made an extra-long spear sheathed with

Opposite: A mound called the Mote was the haunt of the worm at Dalry in the Glenkens (Dumfries and Galloway), and he twined himself round it regularly, until killed by the local blacksmith.

iron to protect himself against the dragon's poison-laden breath; the Walmsgate (Lincolnshire) dragon 'venomed men and beasts with his aire'; the St Leonard's Forest dragon gave off a venom which killed 'both Men and Cattell'; the Mordiford dragon had poisonous breath which finally killed his slayer; and the Nunnington or Loschy Hill worm (North Yorkshire) emitted a poisonous vapour which was absorbed by the dog helping Sir Peter Loschy to kill the dragon. The dog then licked the knight's face, and both died together. This deadly poison, which affected all who ventured too near (and which seems to have been wrongly interpreted, or perhaps more picturesquely interpreted, as fiery breath in paintings and retellings of dragon-killing exploits), taken in conjunction with the whole story of a rampaging monster causing chaos and destruction to land, cattle, and inhabitants, could well be a folk memory of a misuse of or tampering with the potent earth currents, causing disastrous consequences until the situation could be corrected by someone with the necessary specialist knowledge or abilities (that is, until the dragon could be killed by a skilful hero).

Allegorical dragon traditions

The study of dragon lore is an involved one, and no one has as yet completely managed to disentangle the fact, fiction, and folklore. What is clear is that all dragon stories cannot be interpreted literally. As stated earlier, when we put forward seven possible explanations for dragon traditions, each case is individual, and while some may represent genuine visitations by as yet unidentified creatures, others may be purely allegorical. Evidence for the allegorical nature of at least some of the traditions is given by J. Harland and T. T. Wilkinson in their book *Lancashire Legends*:

There is a singular circumstance connected with most of these dragon stories which is worthy of special notice. It is that of the frequent use of *sacred* and *mystic* numbers in the narratives, and this in some degree supports the conjecture that they are allegorical in their nature. In the case of the Dragon of Wantley (Wharncliffe) there are *seven* heads mentioned, and twice *seven* eyes; the monster itself ate up *three* children, the fight lasted *two* days and *one* night, and he turned twice *three* times round when he received his fatal wound. The Lambton Worm had *nine* holes on each side of his mouth, he encircled Worm hill *three* times, he drank the milk of *nine* cows; the reckless heir of Lambton returned a true knight at the end of *seven* years, and for *nine* generations the sybil's curse remained on his house in consequence of the non-performance of his vow.

This quotation deals with the numerology of dragon traditions (and in fact the significant numbers three, seven and nine reappear elsewhere in

The Christian interpretation of dragon-slaying.

this book, especially Chapter Six), but the allegorical interpretation can take other forms. We have already shown how dragon lore links up with what is known or suspected about the earth currents, and highly relevant to this aspect of dragon lore is the Chinese science of *feng-shui*. This is described by E. J. Eitel in *Feng-Shui* and by John Michell in *The View Over Atlantis* and *The Earth Spirit*, but briefly it was the study and interpretation of lines of magnetism which cover the surface of the earth. The magnetic force was known as the dragon current, its paths as the dragon paths or *lung-mei*, and in China buildings, especially tombs, and trees, posts, and stones, were carefully positioned following the advice of geomancers. The *lung-mei* of China sound remarkably like the leys of Britain; the dragon current flowing along the *lung-mei* might have its counterpart in the earth current which, as the traditions in this book show, has flowed and maybe is still flowing through Britain's ancient sites. The dragons of Britain's folklore personify this current; when it is misused, the dragon gets out of control and must be killed.

There is another allegorical interpretation of dragon traditions, and especially dragon-killings, which is more familiar to most people through the stories of St George and St Michael. Today the Church conventionally interprets these traditions as symbolising the battle between the forces of good and evil, with the ultimate triumph of the good Christian over the evil dragon or serpent. There can be no doubt that the Christian missionaries to these islands found great difficulty in making headway against the established practices, though they made determined efforts to eradicate paganism (as described more fully in Chapter Five). But it was many centuries before the country could be considered Christian, and there was probably considerable localised strife between the two factions which sometimes became embodied in stories of dragon-slayings. Significance is found in the siting of some dragon-killings, such as those at Sockburn and Brinsop, which are both very close to old churches. Many hilltops throughout the country are associated with St Michael and often have churches on their summits dedicated to him, especially notable being St Michael's Mount and Glastonbury Tor. These hilltops were the sacred sites of the earlier race and it was here that the life-giving serpent power was invoked; and so these sites became the objective of the Christian campaign and the newer deity supplanted the old, whose influence and significance began to wane. St Michael had successfully killed the dragon.

4 The giant's apron and the Devil's spade

The belief occurs in a great number of folk stories that many ancient structures and also some of the more unusual natural features of our landscape were constructed or placed in position by some superhuman agent, usually a giant or the Devil, occasionally a witch or a fairy. As will be seen later in this chapter, the same themes recur frequently, and the choice of agent seems arbitrary. In fact for our purposes the agent is irrelevant: it is the beliefs that led these stories to develop that are important. The possible meanings of these stories, and their connection with the idea of earth currents, will be explored later; but first, a short digression into giantlore to show that a belief in giants was part of the fabric of tradition.

The twelfth-century chronicler Geoffrey of Monmouth wrote in his *History of the Kings of Britain* that at the time when Brutus landed in England, 'the name of the island was Albion, and of none was it inhabited save only of a few giants'. He also told how the famous giant Gogmagog was finally defeated by Corineus, a champion wrestler, and it is these two whose effigies can still be seen in London's Guildhall (they are wrongly known now as Gog and Magog). Two other giants still visible in the British Isles are the figures cut into the southern chalk slopes—the Long Man of Wilmington in East Sussex, and the Cerne Abbas giant in Dorset. Both are of early origin, but no one really knows when or why they were cut. Among the several traditions relating to them has been the explanation that both figures are the memorials of once-living giants, who were killed and their bodies outlined as they lay dead.

A giant of a man whose memorial takes the form of a huge gravestone nearly eight feet long was Tom Hickathrift, defender of the Norfolk Marshland. Stories about his exploits, depicting his superhuman strength, his ability to defeat other giants (he killed the fearful giant of Smeeth), and his kindness to people in trouble, were transmitted orally and by chapbook for many centuries. His supposed gravestone can be seen in the churchyard of Tilney All Saints, near the south wall of the church. Tom stood on a river bank three miles away and threw a stone, saying he wished to be buried where it fell. Rather conveniently, it landed in the churchyard! A similar feature is part of the legend of Jack o' Legs, a robber-giant who lived in a wood at Weston in Hertfordshire, where he acted as a Robin Hood by robbing the rich to give to the poor. His reputed grave is in Weston churchyard, and the following description of it, and of Jack himself, comes from Salmon's *History of Hertfordshire* (1728):

In the churchyard are two Stones, or rather Stumps of Stones at about fourteen Foot asunder, which the Swains will have to be on the Grave of a Giant. It is not improbable that they belonged to two several Graves, to the Head or Feet of both. About 70 years ago a very long Thigh-bone was taken out of the Church

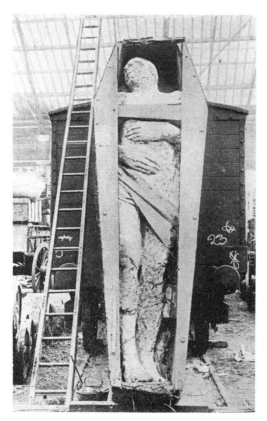

The 'fossilized Irish giant'.

chest, where it had lain many years for a Shew, and sold by the Clerk to John Trediskin, who, we are told, put it amongst the rarities of Oxford.

This Giant, called Jack o' Legs, as Fame goes, lived in a wood here, was a great Robber, but a generous one, for he plundered the Rich to feed the Poor. He took bread from the Baldock Bakers frequently, who taking him at an advantage, put out his Eyes and after hanged him upon a Knoll in Baldock Field. He made them at his Exit but one single Request, which they granted: that he might have his Bow put into his Hand, and wherever his Arrow fell he should be buried, which happened to be in Weston churchyard.

A variation on the bow and arrow story says that Jack requested that a chapel should be built where the arrow landed. It flew four miles, to the site where Weston church now stands—in proof of the story! This version has similarities to some of the tales of church siting given in Chapter Five.

To conclude this brief incursion into the realm of 'real' giants, here is an extract from the *Strand Magazine* for December 1895. Whether the reader accepts the genuineness of this giant or not is up to him. We know nothing more than is given in the following account.

Pre-eminent among the most extraordinary articles ever held by a railway company is the fossilized Irish giant, which is at this moment lying at the London and North-Western Railway Company's Broad-street goods depot, and a photograph of which is reproduced here. This monstrous figure is reputed to have been dug up by a Mr. Dyer whilst prospecting for iron ore in Co. Antrim. The principal measurements are: Entire length, 12ft. 2in.; girth of chest, 6ft 6½in.; and length of arms, 4ft. 6in. There are six toes on the right foot. The gross weight is 2 tons 15 cwt.; so that it took half a dozen men and a powerful crane to place this article of lost property in position for the *Strand Magazine* artist. Dyer, after showing the giant in Dublin, came to England with his queer find and exhibited it in Liverpool and Manchester at sixpence a head, attracting scientific men as well as gaping sightseers. Business increased and the showman induced a man named Kershaw to purchase a share in the concern. In 1876, Dyer sent this giant from Manchester to London by rail; the sum of £4 2s. 6d. being charged for carriage by the company, but never paid. Evidently Kershaw knew nothing of the removal of the 'show', for when he discovered it he followed in hot haste, and, through a firm of London solicitors, moved the Court of Chancery to issue an order restraining the company from parting with the giant, until the action between Dyer and himself to determine the ownership was disposed of. The action was never brought to an issue.

One comment we would make concerning the photograph. It is not clear whether the drapery around the figure was there when the giant was found, or was added later for the sake of decorum, but it looks an unlikely kind of garment, so if it could be ascertained that the material was also 'fossilized', then this would of course be a strong indication that the whole thing was a hoax—if the behaviour of the parties involved does not indicate that already.

The last resting-place of the legendary Jack o' Legs.

One of the Gogmagog figures inside London's Guildhall.

Formation and positioning of ancient structures

Both man-made ancient sites, recognised by archaeologists as being relics of early man, and those formations of rocks and hills that are generally considered to be natural, have traditions attached to them relating how they were formed by giants, the Devil, or other supernatural powers. Though the natural formations are not recognised as 'ancient sites', the fact that the traditions exist suggests that these geographical features had a significance for early man, and so we have included some of these stories in the section which follows the present one, in order to give a more complete picture of the possible extent of early man's effect upon the formation of the earth's surface.

One of Cornwall's many giants was responsible for the building of Treryn Castle, an Iron Age cliff castle near Porthcurno. He sat one night on the promontory and raised the castle from the sea. He also placed an egg-shaped stone in a hole in the rock, and said that if anyone removed it the castle and promontory would fall into the sea. The stone is said to be still there, but the way to it lies along a dangerous ledge, and although the stone is loose in its hole, it cannot be removed. Also in Cornwall, an earth bank about seven miles long is attributed variously to the Devil and Jack the Giant Killer; the name of the bank is Giant's Hedge. We have seen two versions of a rhyme about it:

> Jack the giant had nothing to do,
> So he made a hedge from Lerrin to Looe.   *Or*

> One day the Devil, having nothing to do,
> Built a great hedge from Lerrin to Looe.

Spinsters' Rock, Drewsteignton (Devon) is said to have been erected by three spinsters (spinning women) one morning before breakfast, to amuse themselves when they were taking their spun wool to the collecting agent.

Other similar earthworks elsewhere in the country are also said to have superhuman origins, for example the Devil's Dyke, a Saxon defensive earthwork which runs seven miles from Reach Fen to Wood Ditton in Cambridgeshire. This is said to have been built by the Devil or giants, and the Devil also constructed Offa's Dyke, the earth bank and ditch which still runs most of the length of the Welsh/English border, though not precisely on the line of the present border. He completed this stupendous task in one night, using a plough pulled by a turkey and a gander. A barrow called Hangour Hill, at Swaffham in Norfolk, was formed as a literal offshoot of one of the Devil's ditch-digging exercises. He cleaned his spade against a tree, and the barrow is the lump of earth which fell off.

In Scotland, an unusual man-made cave is attributed to giants, who are said to have constructed it in one night. It is the Cave of Raitts, or the Great Cave (An Maimbr Mhor) near Lynchat (Highland: Inverness), which is usually identified as a Picts' house of the fifth century AD. Horseshoe-shaped, the cave is seventy feet long, eight feet broad and seven feet high, and the roof is formed of large stone slabs. The giantesses who dug out the cave carried the earth in their aprons down to the River Spey where they dumped it; the giants, meanwhile, were quarrying stones in the hills, ready for insertion in the cave as soon as the excavation work was finished.

A considerable amount of this folklore relates to stones that were thrown somewhere for a specific purpose; though sometimes they fell accidentally when the agent was carrying them. The Druid's Lapfu', a standing stone at Yevering in Glendale (Northumberland), was being carried by a druid in his apron (why or where is not stated) when the apron-string broke and the stone fell to the ground. The broken apron-string theme recurs in the next section, and one can only conclude that the Devil, giants, and others were buying an inferior brand of apron!

Longstone is a group of houses in St Mabyn parish (Cornwall), and the name comes from a granite monolith which stood nearby. (It has been used to make four large gateposts and the spans for a small bridge—a fate which many other standing stones have suffered over the centuries.) The stone was originally the Devil's whetstone, thrown in a fit of anger at the smith of St Mabyn. The two were settling their differences in a trial of strength, each trying to reap an acre of corn in the shortest time. The smith had cunningly concealed harrow-tines (sharp spikes) in the Devil's acre, with the result that the Devil had to keep stopping to sharpen his scythe. He threw his whetstone at the smith and flew off, and while the stone stood erect in the ground he did not return. Since a farmer felled it, he has returned to haunt the neighbourhood, or so the story goes.

Also resulting from a burst of anger is the standing stone La Longue Rocque (also known as the Fairy's Battledore) at St Peter in the Wood, Guernsey (Channel Islands). The fairy Le Grand Colin stuck it in the ground during a game of shuttlecock and battledore with his son, who complained about Le Grand Colin hitting the shuttlecock too far away. The beings responsible for the siting of stones seem to have been fond of playing games with them, and they were especially fond of quoits, which is mentioned frequently in these tales. The Hell-stone, a dolmen on Black-

The Devil's Dyke near Brighton (East Sussex) was started as a channel to the sea, part of the Devil's scheme to drown all the people of Sussex to put an end to their religious fervour. He abandoned his plan when the dyke was half completed, when, seeing an old woman's candle, he thought it was the sunrise and fled.

Mol Walbee's Stone, which now stands inside Llowes church.

down near Portesham (Dorset), was thrown there by the Devil from Portland, nine miles or so away, when he was playing quoits. Jack o' Kent, a Herefordshire giant, was playing peck and toss (pitch and toss) on the Sugar Loaf Mountain when he threw what became known as the Pecked Stone into a field at Trelleck (Gwent). This stone lay a short distance from three other tall menhirs (Harold's Stones) which were thrown by Jack at the same time and which still stand together in a field just outside the village. A giant and a dwarf had a stone-throwing competition near Strathpeffer (Highland: Ross and Cromarty). Near the old church of Fodderty (now a house), three standing stones can be seen, one of which, the Eagle Stone, has an eagle carved on it. This stone, too heavy to be lifted by three men, was thrown by a giant from the hills near by; whereupon the dwarf picked up in turn two standing stones (too heavy for *seven* men), which had been the gateposts of the old fort of Knockfarrel, and threw them after the Eagle Stone.

Another recurring theme is the pebble in the shoe, the pebble, however, being of huge proportions to our eyes. Arthur's Stone is a cromlech stand-to go, was in a bad mood when he met the old man, and asked him the distance to Devizes. The old man said he had left there three years ago, and showed the sack of old boots, which he said he had worn out since leaving the town, whereupon the Devil threw down his load of earth in anger, and disappeared. Thus was Silbury Hill formed. Another version tells how the Devil was planning to drop a pile of earth on Avebury because he couldn't stand the amount of religion practised there. But the prayers and spells of the priests, who saw him coming, stopped him from reaching the village, and he dropped his load not far away, where Silbury Hill now stands.

A variation on the 'bag of shoes' story comes from Shobdon (Hereford and Worcester), which was saved from the Devil's wrath by the quick thinking of a cobbler. The Devil was displeased by the fact that the village was a happy place, with a fine church, and he determined to destroy it. About to enter the village, he asked a cobbler, whom he saw carrying a bag of shoes, if this was Shobdon. To which the cobbler replied, 'No, I am seeking the same place, and have worn out all these shoes, but cannot find it in this direction. You had better turn back.' Which the Devil did, apparently also abandoning his plan, because he dropped his load of earth at the entrance to the village, and the mound became known as the Devil's Shovelful.

It was the giant Gorm who was responsible for Maes Knoll, a hilltop camp at Norton Malreward (Avon). For some unexplained reason he was carrying a shovelful of earth around and stumbled at the edge of the Cotswolds. The soil fell into the Avon valley, forming Maes Knoll, and the nearby linear earthwork Wansdyke was formed when the giant dug his shovel into the ground. The disturbance to his valley caused by the dropping of Maes Knoll displeased the Lord of Avon, and clumsy Gorm tripped over his own feet as he ran away from the Lord's wrath. He fell into the Bristol Channel and was drowned, his bones forming the two islands Steep Holme and Flatholme.

Formation of natural features

The stories telling how the ancient stones and mounds came to be placed contain themes which are repeated in traditions explaining the formation of natural landscape features. Again we find the supernatural intervention of giants and t e Devil, with shovelfuls of earth, broken apron-strings, games of quoits, and stone projectiles. We have collected over one hundred of these tales, but as our present concern is the folklore of *ancient sites* we will quote only a few of the more unusual and interesting stories—which nevertheless do have a relevance to our enquiry into earth currents, as will be seen at the end of the chapter.

Pyon Hill (right) and Butthouse Knapp (Hereford and Worcester) are also called Robin Hood's Butts, and there is a story that these two hills were formed by Robin Hood and Little John as the result of a wager.

The tales containing variations on the 'shovelful of earth' theme are perhaps the most intriguing. The most-quoted story tells how a Welsh giant was planning to dam the River Severn and flood Shrewsbury (Salop), and was on his way with a load of earth when he met a cobbler who thwarted his plan in the usual cunning way. The soil the giant threw down became the Wrekin, and Wenlock Edge (or, in another version, Ercall Hill) was formed where he scraped his boots. The Devil formed Cley Hill near Warminster (Wiltshire) with the soil he had intended to throw over Devizes, but in this case he was led astray by an old man who said that his hair had turned grey during the years he had been searching for that town. Another new twist to this theme comes in the stories of the hills Pyon Hill and Butthouse Knapp near Canon Pyon (Hereford and Worcester). Robin Hood and Little John were each carrying a spadeful of earth with the intention of burying the monks at Wormsley, but a cobbler used the 'worn shoes trick' on them and they fell for it. In another version, the Devil was intending to destroy Hereford, but was thwarted by an ecclesiastic he met on the way. Yet another story attributes these two hills to a wager between Robin Hood and Little John. As they stood together at Brinsop, Robin Hood said he could jump over Wormsley Hill to Canon Pyon—but when he did so he knocked a piece out of the hill, which became Butthouse Knapp. When Little John jumped, he also kicked the hill, and Pyon Hill was formed in this way. Finally, the story of Cnwc Coedfoel, a mound near Llandyssul (Dyfed: Cardigan). The Devil was out to drown the people of Pentre-Cwrt (Dyfed: Carmarthen) by damming the River Teivy with earth, but as he was carrying his shovelful he met a cobbler at Llandyssul, two miles from Pentre-Cwrt, who showed him his large bundle of old shoes as evidence of the enormous distance to the river. This discouraged the Devil, who threw down his load. He must have been very easily discouraged, for one would have thought that his ability to take giant strides (as he must have been able, if he could carry shovelfuls of earth as big as Silbury Hill) would have caused him to laugh off any cobbler's 'evidence' as to the distance of his goal!

One 'apron-string' story will suffice to illustrate this theme which again is widespread: the heaps of rocks supposedly dropped when a giant's apron-string broke are often called by some relevant name, such as the Apron String near Mullion (Cornwall), the Giantess's Apronful, which is the passage-grave Barclodiad y Gawres on Anglesey (Gwynedd), the Devil's Apronful on Pock Stones Moor (North Yorkshire, between Nidderdale and Wharfedale), and the Great Apronful and the Little Apronful near Ilkley (West Yorkshire). The giant Cormoran and his wife Cormelian were building a stonghold in the forest that has since flooded to form Mount's Bay near Marazion (Cornwall). They were using white granite, which had to be fetched some distance, and the giants carried the rocks in their aprons. One day, Cormelian saw that her husband was asleep, so she went and got stone from a much nearer source. She was carrying a large piece of this greenstone in her apron when Cormoran awoke. He immediately saw what was happening and, having insisted that only white granite be used, he kicked his wife. Her apron-string broke, the rock fell to the ground, and Cormelian ran away. Alone Cormoran finished the building of what is now St Michael's Mount, and the greenstone rock (called Chapel Rock) can still be seen beside the causeway leading across the bay to the mount.

The importance of one type of stone for a particular purpose, to the exclusion of all others, is not unique to this story. There are many examples of prehistoric monuments built of a type of rock not found in the immediate area, and therefore presumably especially imported, the most famous being Stonehenge's bluestones. Why this should be so is open to conjecture, but it is very possible that it had some relevance to the operation of these monuments as power-generators or power-stores, and this idea will be discussed more fully in Chapter Six.

The Blind Fiddler, turned to stone for disregarding the Sabbath.

Men turned to stone, or the not-so-merry maidens

Not all the traditions relating how ancient stone structures were
formed involve giants or the Devil. There is a whole group of tales
describing how men and women were turned to stone for various mis-
demeanours, a number of them indiscretions provoking the disapproval of
Christians, such as a non-religious activity practised on a Sunday. In
Cornwall, there are several sites illustrating this theme, for example the
Hurlers on Bodmin Moor, three stone circles composed of 'men trans-
form'd into stones, for playing at ball [the traditional Cornish sport of
hurling] on Sunday' (Camden, 1587). The Merry Maidens, a stone circle

in St Buryan parish, were a group of young girls who, walking in the fields one Sabbath evening, began to dance to the music of two pipers (evil spirits in disguise), and were turned into stone in a flash of lightning. The pipers did not escape the girls' fate, and two tall standing stones known as the Pipers can be seen in neighbouring fields. The Nine Maidens and the Fiddler at Wadebridge similarly illustrate the folly of preferring dancing outdoors to attendance at church; and the Blind Fiddler, an impressive standing stone at Catchall, near Penzance, suffered the fate of eternal petrifaction for playing his fiddle on a Sunday.

The names Merry Maidens and Nine Maidens occur elsewhere in the country, and although no traditions are recorded, it is probable that the same one was once told of these sites too. The Nine Maidens on Belstone Common near Okehampton (Devon) were petrified for dancing on a Sunday, and they are said to dance daily at noon. It has been suggested that the 'Nine' of 'Nine Maidens', 'Nine Stones', etc., does not refer to the number of stones, and in fact personal observation has shown that at sites called by these names, the number of stones is rarely nine. 'Nine' comes from 'none' or 'noon', which was originally 3 p.m. and the ninth hour of the day in Roman and ecclesiastical reckoning. Later, when the church service called Nones was moved to midday, 'noon' came to mean our mid-day. The naming of stones with the word 'Nine' may be linked to the belief that they turned at midday (an aspect of stone lore which is described more fully in Chapter Six), as exemplified by the Nine Stones at Belstone which are said to dance at noon. Another theory was advanced by T. C. Lethbridge in his book *Witches*. This proposes that originally the 'Great Mother' goddess, symbolised by the moon, was worshipped at the site and that later she evolved into deities with the attributes of the new moon, the full moon, and the waning moon. Then still later these three goddesses were again seen as having three aspects each, thereby making nine god-desses or maidens. More prosaic is the idea that 'Nine Maidens' comes from the Cornish *Naw Men* (nine stones), or, as there are rarely nine stones, from *Maidn Nun* (moorland stones).

Other examples of petrifaction for dancing on a Sunday come from wide-spread areas of the British Isles: Devon, where a pile of rocks in the Valley of Rocks near Lynton is all that is left of Ragged Dick and his dancing companions; South Glamorgan, where the stones of Tinkinswood chambered cairn, Dyffryn, were women dancers turned to stone; Shetland, where the stones of a circle in Fetlar called Haltadans are trows or trolls caught dancing at sunrise, along with a fiddler and his wife, now two stones in the centre of the circle; and County Wicklow, where the Piper's Stones at Athgreany, Hollywood, are a circle and standing stone repre-senting dancers and a piper. Stonehenge (Wiltshire) too may possibly once have had the same tradition attached to it, for an early name for the

The Cove at Stanton Drew contains three stones said to be a parson, a bride-groom, and his bride.

Opposite: Long Meg (on the skyline) and her Daughters.

monument, according to twelfth-century scholar Alexander Neckam, was Chorea Gigantum, or the Giants' Dance.

The most detailed petrifaction story involving desecration of the Sabbath relates to the stone circles and other megaliths at Stanton Drew (Avon). These were described as follows by Dr William Stukeley, the eighteenth-century antiquarian:

This noble monument is vulgarly called the Weddings; and they say, 'tis a company that assisted at a nuptial solemnity thus petrify'd. In an orchard near the church is a cove consisting of three stones like that of the northern circle in Abury or that of Long Stones, this they call the parson, the bride, and bride-groom.

The trouble began when the wedding, which had been celebrated throughout the Saturday, looked like continuing into the Sunday. The fiddler who was playing for the dancing refused to continue after midnight, and as if in answer to the dancers' pleas, a dark-clad stranger suddenly appeared and began to play. The music was hypnotic, and as it went faster and faster so too did the dancers, for they were unable to stop. At dawn, the music ceased, and the fiddler, who was of course the Devil, said he would return some day and play for them again. So far, he has not kept his promise, and until he does they must all remain in petrified form. Only the original fiddler was saved—he was found next morning hiding under a hedge.

It has been suggested that the transgression of dancing on the Sabbath does not relate to Sunday at all, 'Sabbath' being a mistake for the witches' 'Sabbat'. As support for this idea, Long Meg and her Daughters, a large circle with a tall outlying standing near Little Salkeld (Cumbria), was described as a coven of witches turned to stone by a magician. And the numerous merry maidens, as well as the wedding party at Stanton Drew, had musical accompaniment on the pipe or fiddle by a man sometimes described as the Devil, a feature common to reports of witches' gatherings.

Other transgressions of the Sabbath were also punished by the rather severe penalty of petrifaction, such as winnowing (three stones formerly on Moelfre Hill, Dwygyfylchi, Gwynedd: Caernarvon, representing three women dressed in red, white, and blue gowns—the stones were a dull red, white, and a slate colour—who worked on a Sunday morning despite the protestations of their neighbours), shearing sheep (stones at Grievestead Farm, Grindon, Northumberland), and working in a turnip field (Duddo Stones, Duddo, Lowick, Northumberland). A man who stole the church Bible (an alternative version says the church bells) was turned to stone as he carried it away on his back, and he must stand there for ever (or at least until the last trump sets him free)—the Robber's Stone (Carreg y Lleidr) is a standing stone which from a certain angle resembles a hump-backed man, and it stands near Llandyfrydog on the island of Anglesey (Gwynedd). The tall standing stones of Callanish on Lewis (Western Isles) are said to be the old giant inhabitants of Lewis who refused to be christened or to build a church when Christianity was introduced to the isles. They were turned to stone by St Kieran, who had come to preach to them.

Transgression of the Sabbath and animosity towards Christianity were not always the reasons for the fate of eternal petrifaction, however, and a variety of other reasons are given in the following tales. A group of standing stones near Cottrell in South Glamorgan was said to represent some women who had caused an innocent man to be hanged because they had sworn falsely against him. Near Chapel Garioch (Grampian: Aberdeen), a girl fleeing from the unwanted embrace of a warlock was turned to stone,

Three stones in Kilross parish (Sligo), formerly a cow, a boy, and a thief. The cow was stolen from a magician by a neighbour and his son, and the magician turned them all to stone by striking them with his magic wand as soon as he caught up with them.

Overleaf: The King's Men stand silent in the dawn light, as they have stood for years without number.

now the Maiden Stone, as he seized her. She was praying for deliverance, which came in an unexpected and somewhat final form. (It has also been suggested that the petrifaction of dancers was sometimes considered as a relief from eternal dancing rather than as a punishment.) Three stones on a beach on the island of Inisbofin (Donegal) represent a white cow, a witch, and a fisherman, turned to stone miraculously for no apparent reason. The fisherman, landing on the island by accident, saw the witch drive the cow into a lake and strike it with a wand, whereupon it turned to stone. In his anger at this, he struck the witch, and they both turned to stone. The Druid's Circle near Killarney (Kerry) consists of a circular embankment containing seven upright stones, with two larger stones outside. The latter were two giants and the seven smaller stones were their sons, all turned to stone by Donald Egeelagh, a prince and enchanter who was at war with the giants and unable to defeat them in any way other than this. Seven boulders on a circular rampart which surrounds the tumulus Cruckancornia, in the townland of Scurmore, Castleconnor parish (Sligo), are known as the Children of the Mermaid. She turned them into stone

when she returned to the sea after many years as the wife of a human man.

A story of a rather different kind tells how the Rollright Stones in Oxfordshire came into being. A king was riding across the county when he was met by a witch who said:

> Seven long strides thou shalt take,
> And if Long Compton thou canst see,
> King of England thou shalt be.

His knights stood together in a huddle, and his soldiers waited close by, as the king strode out to fulfil the prophecy. In excitement he cried:

> Stick, stock, stone!
> As King of England I shall be known!

But alas, his view was blocked by the Archdruid's Barrow, and the witch decreed:

> As Long Compton thou canst not see,
> King of England thou shalt not be,
> Rise up stick, and stand still stone,
> For King of England thou shalt be none.
> Thou and thy men hoar stones shall be,
> And I myself an eldern-tree.

The king and his men are there still, waiting for the spell to be broken. The king stands apart, a huge rearing stone, the King Stone, now encased in iron railings. His soldiers form the circle the King's Men, while the Whispering Knights, a separate group of five stones (actually the remains of a burial chamber) can be seen across the field. A story similar to this may once have been told in Northamptonshire, where the following saying relates to a spring called Padwell and a stone called the Horestone, near Edgcott:

> If we can Padwell overgo and Horestone we can see,
> Then lords of England we shall be.

It is of course not only prehistoric monuments which are the end-products of petrifaction, just as it is not always human beings who are petrified. We have already mentioned cows more than once, and cattle also feature in a tale from the island of Mull (Strathclyde), where a glaistig (supernatural being) attached to the Lamont family at Ardnadrochit turned their cattle into stones to avoid their being stolen. The grey stones are to be seen in the Heroes' Hollow (Glaic nan Gaisgeach). In Gloucester-

The Eglone was traditionally known to be a giant turned to stone by a magician who had a dispute with him. This huge block of limestone, nearly eighteen feet high, is at Moytirra, near Highwood, overlooking Lough Arrow in County Sligo.

shire, a group of large stones called the Grey Geese on a hill at Addlestrop were once live geese being taken to market (or, in some tales, pasture) by their owner. A witch stopped her and asked for money, and on being refused turned the geese into stones. Two huge and prominent granite boulders on the summit of Corn Ridge near Sourton village (Devon) are known as Branscombe's Loaf and Cheese, and represent these two items of food which on a long journey were offered to Walter Branscombe, Bishop of Exeter, by a mysterious stranger, who was the Devil. The bishop's servant realised this, and knocked the food from his master's hand before he had time to eat any of it. A saddle-shaped stone by the Saddle-road near Braddan on the Isle of Man was a saddle used on the vicar's horse one night by a little man in a green jacket; and the Sack Stone, Fonaby (Lincolnshire) was a sack of corn turned to stone by Christ. Riding through the fields on an ass, he saw men sowing corn, and asked for grain for his ass. They did not recognise him and said they had no grain. When he asked what was in the sack, they told him 'Stones', and his reply was, 'Stone be it!'

Landscape engineering

What do all these strange tales mean? Some were undoubtedly born of a fertile imagination, inspired by the sight of stones in weird shapes and groupings. But the majority of these apparently ridiculous stories could refer to a time when stones and mounds were positioned in a particular location as part of a countrywide plan to make maximum use of the natural earth currents. If this was so, then tales of giants and others throwing stones around could simply be an interpretation of an activity which had become incomprehensible to a later race.

How intensive the 'landscape engineering' may have been is not possible to judge, though traditions such as that relating to the mountains of what used to be called Sutherland suggest the possibility that early man did

The Sutherland skyline, with Suilven on the left. Norse gods were said to be responsible for the strange shapes of Sutherland's mountains.

more than simply move relatively small stones and mounds of earth around. Many of Sutherland's mountains, such as Quinag, Suilven, and the Stack, are weird shapes, and it is told how they were modelled by the Norse gods who came here to practise their craft when the world was new. Having gained experience, they returned home to model the mountains of Norway. A number of the tales included in this chapter relate to earth-moving enterprises, some on a large scale such as Silbury Hill and the Wrekin, and some of the stories which we have not quoted for lack of space include explanations of how such relatively large features as Cheddar Gorge, the Scilly Isles, the Giant's Causeway, and Loch Ness came into being. This group of large landscaped features could also include the suggested terrestrial zodiac at Glastonbury in Somerset, which covers a circular area ten miles across. Here the signs of the zodiac are said to be depicted by outlines formed by waterways (natural and man-made), old trackways, modern roads, and field boundaries, with hills and earthworks sometimes falling in significant positions (for example, the linear earthwork Ponter's Ball forms the horn of the Capricorn goat; the tree-covered tumulus Wimble Toot is the nipple of the Virgo figure; and high ground at Compton Dundon, rising from the flat surrounding land, forms the Gemini figure). If this zodiac really does exist on the ground as well as in the minds of its protagonists, and if the other suggested zodiacs elsewhere in Britain (which are at the moment, however, less well investigated and documented) are also a reality, then this would be further evidence that at some time in the past carefully planned landscape engineering on a very large scale was carried out.

Guy Underwood claims in *The Pattern of the Past* that dowsing reveals that such large-scale landscape alteration was indeed performed.

We have become so accustomed to the facile explanation that the strange banks, ditches, mounds, pits, coombs, unlikely shaped hilltops, and rocks (often balanced upon each other) found in uncultivated places are due to the 'surge and swirl of primeval waters,' or to glacial erosion, or earthquakes, that it is difficult to admit the possibility that the greater part of the minor topography of the land, and some of its major features such as the Dartmoor Tors and the Grey Wethers, might be artificial and religious in origin, as is established by geodetic survey.

He gives further examples of major features which have been altered by man, such alterations being done in order to mark important geodetic features. On a smaller scale, he says that geodetic phenomena, which 'were accepted as divine manifestations of the Life Spirit', were marked by visible man-made symbols.

Because these phenomena were complicated and invisible, it was natural that priests should evolve some system whereby they could be rendered recognizable to the initiated, while still remaining incomprehensible to outsiders. They did this by means of mounds, banks, ditches, stones, dolmens, stone circles, walls, terraces, roads, pits, and ponds in varying arrangements. Thirty kinds of such topographical markings were used by ancient man. Each signified a different geodetic phenomenon or pattern, and sites with special significance were thus marked.

To do this must have involved a vast amount of physical labour, and Underwood himself states that not everyone would understand what was being done—'whereby they could be rendered recognizable to the initiated, while still remaining incomprehensible to outsiders'. All the tales in this chapter could be explained in this way, as attempts by the uninitiated to rationalise incomprehensible happenings. The apparently ridiculous nature of the tales has kept them alive over the centuries, and so today we have in much garbled form an account of landscape engineering thousands of years ago.

5 Churches moved by night

Paganism versus Christianity

Worship at prehistoric monuments continued in many forms long after the disintegration of the powerful practices of the early civilisations who initiated the stone circles and other megalithic structures. Some of the distorted forms of this 'worship' have already been described in this book. We cannot be sure of the exact nature of the religion practised in the British Isles at the time when Christianity was first introduced, but there is considerable evidence to suggest that it was a form of Nature worship, and that the much-maligned witchcraft was at its core. Some writers have attempted to trace the early origins of witchcraft, and if one can forget the twentieth-century preoccupation with black magic (which is a comparatively recent innovation), it becomes clear that the real witchcraft is more than likely to be yet another variation on the ways in which the old practices were perpetuated. More will be said concerning witches and their links with ancient sites in Chapter Seven.

At the time of the introduction of Christianity to these islands, the missionaries were not greeted by a people searching for a new religion. As were missionaries in the more recent past, they were faced with the task of weaning the natives away from their traditional, so-called 'pagan' practices, and had to contend with much spirited opposition. That the Britons and the inhabitants of France (whose prehistory, especially in Brittany, parallels that of the British Isles in many respects) still preferred their old ways to the new is evidenced by the number of edicts which were issued by the Christians concerning the worship of stones. The tone of these indicates that they were annoyed by the failure of the natives gratefully to adopt the benefits of the Christian religion. In the edict of Arles in AD 452 is the statement: 'if any infidel either lighted torches, or worshipped trees, fountains or stones, or neglected to destroy them, he should be found guilty of sacrilege.' The Council of Tours in 567 recommended the excommunication of those who persisted in worshipping trees, stones, or fountains. Evidently these exhortations did not have the desired effect, for stone worship was still a problem one hundred years later. The decree of Nantes in 658 stated that 'Bishops and their servants' should 'dig up and remove and hide to places where they cannot be found, those stones which in remote and woody places are still worshipped and where vows are still made'. The same attitude could still be found in the nineteenth century, 1,200 years later. The people of Manaton (Devon) used to carry coffins three times round the churchyard cross, much to the annoyance of the vicar, who preached against this ritual. It continued, however, so he broke up the cross and hid the pieces.

By the time the decree of Nantes was issued some bishops had realised

Rudston monolith almost overshadows the Christian church within whose precincts it stands.

that it would be necessary to use new tactics in order to subdue the heathen practices of the people. This new attitude was shown in a letter of AD 601, from Pope Gregory to Abbot Mellitus, who was about to visit England.

When (by God's help) you come to our most reverend brother, Bishop Augustine, I want you to tell him how earnestly I have been pondering over the affairs of the English: I have come to the conclusion that the temples of the idols in England should not on any account be destroyed. Augustine must smash the idols, but the temples themselves should be sprinkled with holy water and altars set up in them in which relics are to be enclosed. For we ought to take advantage of well-built temples by purifying them from devil-worship and dedicating them to the service of the true God. In this way, I hope the people (seeing their temples are not destroyed) will leave their idolatry and yet continue to frequent the places as formerly, so coming to know and revere the true God.

The Christians not only absorbed traditional sacred sites into their own, they also christianised the ancient gods, so that, for instance, Brid became St Bridget, St Brigit, or St Bride; Santan (the holy fire) became St Anne; Sinclair (the holy light) became St Clare. They also positioned their feasts to coincide with pre-existing festivals, and in this way they succeeded in obliterating all but the minutest traces of the once so powerful religion of Nature.

But this process took many centuries. As late as 1649 the General Assembly of the Church of Scotland appointed a commission to examine and eliminate the 'Druidical Customs' which were still followed at the 'old places of worship'. In the early years, the missionaries faced great difficulties, not least of them being the problems they experienced when they came to site their churches, as is amply demonstrated by the hundreds of traditions which are still current today. The majority of the stories concerning churches relate to the siting of the buildings, and most tell of how, at dead of night, the building work completed during the day was undone by unknown hands, and the building materials moved to another site, often on a hilltop (though not invariably; sometimes they were moved downhill to marshy ground, and we will discuss this later). Finally the builders would have to agree to the local wishes and build the church on the site which was thus indicated. Such stories almost certainly demonstrate an incompatibility between the desires of the incoming Christians and those of the still-powerful 'pagans', who in some respects were still the more influential. They tolerated the building of the Christians' churches, but it had to be done on their terms. They were fully aware of the importance of the position of a sacred building, and apparently they believed that for it to be completely effective it should stand upon one of the lines of the earth current, or leys. Most pre-Reformation churches are found to lie upon leys, and most are on sites which have geomantic significance.

Sometimes major megalithic structures were actually incorporated in the church building. Examples of this are rare in Britain, but there are several interesting ones elsewhere in Europe. Megalithic tombs now form side chapels of two churches in Portugal—the Anta de Alcobertas, Rio Maior, Extremadura, and the Anta-Capella of San Dionisio. In northern Spain, the church of Santa-Cruz de la Victoria in Gangas de Onis is built on a mound containing a passage grave, the church's altarstone being the tomb's capstone; while in Arrichinaga, also in Spain, a church has been built around the dolmen of San Miguel. Perhaps the most extraordinary example is the Chapelle des Sept-Saints at Plouaret in the French Côtes-du-Nord, the south transept of which is a megalithic tomb sixteen feet long by seven feet wide by five feet high, roofed by two capstones.

In the British Isles, five especially notable examples of churches in very close proximity to ancient structures are in Buckinghamshire, Dorset, Humberside, Dyfed, and Gwynedd. West Wycombe church stands within an Iron Age hillfort at West Wycombe (Buckinghamshire), and a now ruined church of Norman origin is inside the prehistoric henge monument at Knowlton (Dorset). At Ysbyty Cynfyn near Aberystwyth (Dyfed: Cardigan) the church is in a circular churchyard, and several megaliths, probably the remains of a stone circle, can be seen in the wall surrounding it. The stones are too massive for it to be sensibly suggested that they were moved there from elsewhere when the churchyard wall was built. This is the only example we know of where a church definitely appears to have been built within a stone circle, but there are many churches throughout the British Isles which have circular churchyards. These could also once have been the sites of stone circles or henges. It is interesting to note that when a cross-shaped building is added to a circular site, the resulting shape is that of the wheel-cross ⊕ which is a sun symbol. Another example of a pagan sacred site blended with a Christian church is also in Wales, at Llanfairpwllgwyngyll (Gwynedd: Anglesey) where a menhir was found beneath the pulpit of the church. And the fifth example is a gigantic monolith (over twenty-five feet high) in the churchyard and very close to the church at Rudston (Humberside), which indicates that the site was sacred in pre-Christian times. In a number of other places in the British Isles, churches have been built very close to ancient stones or earthworks.

Although superficially it might appear that the Christians finally triumphed, their churches often obliterating the old sacred sites and their missionaries often destroying those stones which were focal points for pagan worship, it may be that the devotees of the old religion never admitted defeat. In a number of churches can be seen to the present day intriguing carvings in wood and stone of what are definitely not subjects from the Christian pantheon, but which probably represent ancient gods or symbolise ancient beliefs and practices. Some of these may be thought obscene, and it is hard to understand why they were not quietly destroyed during past restorations, especially those of the Victorians, which certainly destroyed much atmosphere as well as fabric (perhaps many *were* destroyed then). But fortunately a number remain today, for example the beautifully carved figures around the outside of the church at Kilpeck

(Hereford and Worcester), the green men (a green man is a foliate mask, often of demoniacal appearance, probably representing the spirit of fertility) that can be seen in many churches, the less frequent Sheila-na-gig (a lady in an indelicate posture), and many others. These robust carvings, portraying life and fecundity, may have been the opposite of christianising a church—they may have signified that although this was ostensibly a church dedicated to the Christian religion, in fact the old faith was still practised, the old gods still venerated. The religious leaders of many an isolated community may have played a dual role, sustaining the ancient faith and practices behind the façade of imported and alien rituals. Although this is speculation, there *are* cases where Christian priests were

Many churches still contain carvings of an obviously pagan nature, such as (*below*) twelfth-century Sheila-na-gig at Kilpeck (Hereford and Worcester); (*previous page*) green man carved on an early sixteenth-century bench-end at Crowcombe (Somerset); (*opposite*) a twelfth- or thirteenth-century carving which appears to combine both predominant features of the previous two, from Melbourne (Derbyshire). A fertile vine issues from the mouths of the latter two figures, as it does from the mouth of the carved dragon illustrated in Chapter Three.

known to have condoned, and even actively participated in, non-Christian
ceremonies. If there was not support for the old religion within the Church
at a local level, it is hard to understand why these patently non-Christian
carvings were allowed to remain within Christian buildings.

The folklore of church siting reinforces the idea that there was a conflict between pagan and Christian interests. The following examples are
presented by county because there are so many of them. The similarities
in the tales, and the massive countrywide coverage, indicate that the
Christians found it no easy task to establish their churches. Some of the
traditions contain details of how the final site for a church was actually
chosen, through dreams, voices, visible signs, etc., and John Michell in
The View Over Atlantis suggests that these indicate that divination was
practised in order to determine the most suitable site, 'one where the
spiritual forces of the locality combine to the best advantage'. He also
comments, and we agree entirely, that sites for new churches are no longer
chosen so carefully, the practice of divination having been abandoned, with
the result that 'while our older churches are still capable of use as precise
instruments for spiritual invocation, many of those built in modern times
are nothing more than empty halls'. So it appears to be no accident that so
many pre-Reformation churches fall on leys. The effects of the current that
was formerly utilised at stone circles, standing stones, megalithic tombs, and

Alfriston church.

other sites could also be felt within a Christian church, and on occasion its influence is still apparent today.

Church-siting traditions in the south of England

East Sussex. At Alfriston the fourteenth-century church is sited on an ancient mound on the village green. Originally it was to be built in another field, but every morning the builders found that the previous day's work had been undone, the stones having been miraculously transported to the mound on the green. A wise man noticed four oxen lying on the green with their rumps touching, thus making a cross-shape, and this was thought to be a sign that the church should be built on that spot. The cruciform shape of the bodies of the oxen was echoed in the shape of the church.

Udimore church was to have been built across the River Ree, but the stones were moved over the river every night, and a voice was heard calling 'O'er the mere! O'er the mere!' So the new site over the river was adopted.

There are two explanations of why Hollington church near Hastings was located in a wood. In both versions, the work done by villagers when building the church was undone again at night, the building materials simply disappearing. One version tells how someone came across a newly-built church in a lonely wood, the Devil having decided to make it inaccessible since he was unable to prevent its construction entirely. (In traditions such as these, 'the Devil' must surely be a Christian reference to the followers of the old religion.) In the other version, priests were about to deal with whatever was interfering with the work, when a voice said that if the church were built at his chosen spot, he would offer no further resistance. This was done, and a thick wood quickly grew up to hide the church from general view.

The Devil and St Dunstan argued over Mayfield church, the former pushing over and tilting at an angle the wooden church being built by the latter—who promptly pushed it back. The Devil interfered again when a new church of stone was being built, undoing the day's work every night, but the story is incomplete in that we do not know if the site was in dispute. At any rate, Mayfield does have a church today.

West Sussex. Steyning church was built on a spot chosen by St Cuthman. He was pushing his mother in a wheelbarrow from Devon to Sussex (was this the first sponsored charity stunt?) and intended to build a church at the point where he received a sign. His barrow broke in Steyning, he repaired it and carried on, but it soon broke again and, seeing it was unrepairable, he realised that this was the site for his church.

Hampshire. Christchurch Priory church in the New Forest was to have been built on St Catherine's Hill, but every morning the building materials had been moved down the hill, to a site about a mile to the south. So the workmen built the church at the new site. It was called Christchurch because of a strange workman who joined the builders. He refused meals and pay, and when a beam was cut too short he touched it and it became the right length. He then disappeared, but all knew that he was Christ, the son of a carpenter.

Isle of Wight. Godshill church was moved to its present position by fairies.

Dorset. Round Meadow was to be the site of a new church in Winterbourne Whitechurch, but no crops would grow there because it had been reaped on a Sunday. When the stones laid one day were found the next in another field, the villagers decided the curse on the ground must still be operative, so the church was built on a new site.

When West Dowlish church was burnt down, the villagers tried to build a new one, but the work was undone by night, so they gave in. The development of the tradition here is relatively recent, for the church burned down at the end of the sixteenth or the beginning of the seventeenth

The original site on Chapel Hill can be seen in this photograph of Braunton church, with the ruins of a chapel just visible. Also illustrated (*opposite*) is the roof boss depicting the sign which showed St Brannoc where to build his church.

century. One explanation of the story put forward is that two churches in one parish would mean paying more tithes, so the work was knocked down by the people of East Dowlish.

Folke church near Sherbourne was moved from a wood named Broke to its present position at night as it was being built. Nearby Holnest church was also moved to a new site.

Wiltshire. Salisbury Cathedral was built to replace that at nearby Old Sarum (an ancient earthwork), which was abandoned in the thirteenth

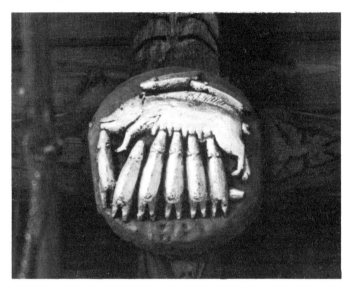

century. Bishop Richard Poore, while searching for a site for his new cathedral in 1220, had a vision of the Virgin who told him to build at Myrfield. He did not know the place, but overheard two labourers talking about it, and they showed him where it was. The new site was on low-lying, marshy ground, close to the River Avon.

A hilltop site was chosen by the Devil for Westwood church (near Bradford-on-Avon), and he moved the stones up there as the church was being constructed on another site.

Somerset. Broadway church is over a mile from the village, amid fields with no houses close by, and no one knows why it should have been built in such an isolated spot. There are several explanations—its site was to have been where the Congregational Chapel now stands, but the materials were carried away at night by the Druids to its present site. Or it might have been the pixies. Or, the chosen site was John Baker's yard, and fairies moved the stones by night. The stones of Curry Mallet church were also moved to a site outside the village; and Glastonbury and Minehead churches have siting traditions, though we do not have the details.

Devon. Chapel Hill was originally intended to be the site for St Brannoc's church at Braunton, but each day's work was demolished by night. St Brannoc saw a sow suckling her piglets in the valley below the hill, and so decided upon this new site for his church. This choice was appropriate, for many of his miracles were concerned with animals. The sow and piglets can be seen on one of the carved roof bossses inside the church, and St Brannoc himself is on one of the sixteenth-century bench-ends.

Buckfastleigh church has over one hundred steps leading up to its hill-top site. It was built there to be out of the Devil's reach, for he had been demolishing by night the building work on the original site on lower ground.

Brentor church on the edge of Dartmoor is one of the bleakest in the country, for it is sited literally on top of a rocky tor. When we visited it a gale was blowing, and the steep grassy path was slippery with rain. Again

One of Britain's bleakest church sites, Brentor.

the Devil is to blame for its location, because he moved it to the tor from lower ground. St Michael (to whom the church is dedicated) appeared when the building was completed and kicked the Devil down the hill, throwing a huge rock after him.

Other Devon churches whose sites were moved are Plympton St Mary, Weare Giffard, and Kibsworthy.

Cornwall. Pulpit was the original site for Talland church, but the work was destroyed by night, and a voice said:

> If you would my wish fulfil,
> Build the church on Talland Hill.

So now the church stands near the sea, away from the centre of the parish.

Altarnun church, the 'cathedral of the moor', had its location chosen by the Devil, who with the assistance of a hare and a deer moved the stones being used in its erection.

At Towednack church, the Devil refused to allow completion of the church tower, and at night undid the day's work on it. The squat tower, without pinnacles or battlements, can still be seen, and there is a local proverb, 'There are no cuckolds in Towednack, because there are no horns on the church tower'.

An unusual story comes from St Mawgan church in Kerrier, which was formerly sited at Carminowe, at the end of the parish. Giants (of whom there were at one time many in Cornwall) used to dig up the dead bodies in the graveyard, so the villagers dug pits and covered them with 'sprouse' (light hay or grass). Unfortunately this attempt to kill the ghouls failed, and so they had to move the church out of the giants' reach. (Though why the giants, who surely had a stride to match their size, could not have walked the extra distance to the new church is not explained, unless the new site had some form of 'psychic barrier' lacking at the first.)

Church-siting traditions in the south and west Midlands

Gloucestershire. Churchdown church is on a steep hill 600 feet above the village, though this was not the site first chosen. Every night the materials used during the day were carried to the top of the hill, until at last the builders gave in.

A field called Church Piece was the original site for Bisley church, but during building the stones were carried mysteriously to the church's present site. During restoration in 1862, a Roman altar with a horseman on it was discovered in the church, and it is thought that this came from

Church Piece, where Roman remains have been found. No one knew of the existence of the altar until its discovery in 1862, but the 'church removal' story was current before then. This indicates that it is possible for folk memory to have a factual basis.

Hereford and Worcester. The original site for Much Cowarne church was on a hill north-east of its present location, but the building materials were continually being moved to the new site, so the church was finally built there. Every night the Devil demolished work done on Kingsland church on a site near Lawton, so a new site was found. The spirits of the dead buried in the churchyard were not pleased when it was decided to rebuild Pencombe church on a new site, so the old site had to be re-used.

When the oxen pulling the hearse containing the body of the murdered St Clodock reached the River Monnow, they refused to go on, and the ropes and chains snapped. This was recognised as a sign from Heaven, so the saint was buried at that spot and a church built over his grave. The village which grew up there is called Clodock.

Warwickshire. In the fourteenth century, a nun called Alice Craft of Wroxall Abbey had a vision of the Virgin, who told her to build a lady chapel by the abbey church. The site would be made known to her. So she engaged workmen, though she had no money. The next morning on going outside, she found 'a certayne ground covered with snow, although it was harvest time, and all the churchyard else bare without snow'. So the workmen began to build the chapel there, and every week Alice found money lying in the churchyard sufficient to pay the workmen and buy the materials.

Oxfordshire. The Devil disapproved of the site chosen for Ambrosden church—in a field called Church Leys—and he moved the building materials to a new site, where the church was finally built. The original site for Checkendon church was to be an old quarry surrounded by yew trees, now called the Devil's Churchyard. But the Devil moved the stones every night to a new site. Another version tells that the stones were moved by a group of villagers who had different ideas about the siting of their church, but that the other villagers believed the Devil was the culprit.

Buckinghamshire. The church at Wendover is nearly half a mile outside the town, because witches carried the stones from the original site nearer the town (still called Witches' Meadow) to the present site.

Hertfordshire. Box, in Stevenage parish, was the original site chosen for the church now at Walkern.

Bedfordshire. There is a separate tower (possibly built as a flood refuge) at Marston Moretaine church, and the Devil is accused of trying to steal it. However it was too heavy for him, so he had to leave it behind.

Salop. A hilltop was chosen for the site of Worfield church, but this did not suit the Devil, who felt it would be too conspicuous with its spire, and would attract too many worshippers. So every night he carried the stones down the hill to the present site.

The first site for Broughton church was on high ground, but again each day's work was mysteriously destroyed and so the people decided to build on lower ground and chose a marshy hollow near Yorton railway station. (The church has now been rebuilt elsewhere.)

Baschurch church was to be built on top of Berth Hill, where there is an ancient earthwork, but the work was nightly undone by no-one-knew-who, and the stones were thrown into Berth Pool at the foot of the hill. 'It' also threw the bells intended for the church into the pool. So a new site was tried, and there was no interference.

At Stoke-upon-Tern the building of the old church (rebuilt 1874) was also interfered with, the stones being carried downhill from the chosen hilltop site to a marsh near the river.

At Wistanstow, in 849, St Wystan was murdered. He was grandson of the King of Mercia, and wished to become 'an heir of a heavenly kingdom' rather than succeed his grandfather. Although his body was buried in Repton, Derbyshire, for '30 days a column of light extending from the spot where he was slain to the heavens above, was seen by all those who dwelt there, and every year, on the day of his martyrdom, the hairs of his head, severed by the sword, sprang up like grass'. A church was built on the spot and pilgrims came to see the hair, but no trace of the Saxon building can now be seen. However, St Wystan and his mother are depicted in one of the stained glass windows of the present church.

Staffordshire. Fairies were blamed for moving the building materials for the church at Hanchurch, near Stoke, so the builders gave in and built on the new site.

West Midlands. Fairies also chose a new site for Walsall church.

Church-siting traditions in the east Midlands and East Anglia

Leicestershire. Breedon-on-the-Hill church stands on a prominent hill, a landmark for miles around. Its site was to have been in the village below, but doves carried the stones to the top of the hill by night. The church contains unique carvings from the Anglo-Saxon monastery formerly on the site; before that, there was an Iron Age hillfort on the hill.

A field now called Churchyard Close, near the Debdale 'side-gate' and two miles from the village, was to have been the site for Kibworth church, but the stones laid by day were removed by night to the church's present location. Despairing of ever getting the church finished, the builders gave in and accepted the new site, whereupon all interruption ceased.

Breedon-on-the-Hill church.

Derbyshire. Clowne church was carried across the road to its present site.

Lincolnshire. Dorrington church is in an isolated spot, the stones having been moved to the site of a 'heathen temple', by demons in Saxon times when it was decided to build a Christian church.

Northamptonshire. In Saxon times the building of a church was begun at the foot of a hill in Church Stowe, in the parish of Stowe-Nine-Churches. But every morning the workmen found their foundations filled in and the stones in the new walls piled up (another version says that the materials were moved to the top of the hill). One night a workman kept watch and saw a monster with a hog-like head ('summat bigger nor a hog') demolishing all the day's work. Eight times they tried to build the church; on the ninth occasion they started building at the top of the hill, and were allowed

Stowe-Nine-Churches church.

to continue unmolested. Other churches in the county which have siting legends are at Great Brington and Oxendon.

Cambridgeshire. The village of Thriplow lies in a hollow, and it was decided to build a church there. The Devil preferred a hilltop site overlooking the village, however, and moved all the stones up to it—so the builders gave in. The Devil also interfered at Cottenham, when the villagers decided to rebuild their church nearer the centre of the village. He nightly removed the stones to the old site at one end of the long village.

At March, the Devil demolished all work on a new church to the north of the River Nene, so the villagers erected a cross to keep him away. They were successful, but even so no church has been built north of the river until more recent times, when the town expanded in that direction. An

The Devil looks pleased with himself as he flies off with Over church. But evil
spirits fear the sound of bells, and the ringing of the Vale Royal abbey church
bells causes Satan to weaken—'As Satan struggled on in pain, His boasted strength
begins to wane', says the 'Legend of Over Church' by Egerton Leigh. 'Stunned
by monks' prayers and pealing noise, In vain he strives the weight to poise:
Swift from his grasp it fell.' Protected by prayer, the church lands unharmed,
and: 'Preserved it stood—there still it stands—Rescued from sacrilegious hands,
Escaped the foul fiend's blow.'

ancient cross base can still be seen in the town.

Norfolk. The detaching of the tower at West Walton church in Norfolk
is attributed to the work of the Devil. He is said to have carried it away
because he objected to the sound of the bells. (All over the world bells
were often rung to keep away evil spirits.) Presumably, as at Marston
Moretaine (Bedfordshire), he found the tower too heavy to carry away
completely, and therefore he failed in his intention.

Suffolk. Another tale involving the Devil and a church tower comes from East Bergholt. The builders of the tower were continually interrupted by the Devil, who pulled down by night what they erected by day, so they hung the bells in a wooden belltower separated from the church.

Essex. The materials being used to build Matching church were moved to a new site.

The legendary pig carved on the west wall of Winwick church.

Church-siting traditions in the north of England

Cheshire. Over church originally stood in the centre of the town, but the Devil carried it off complete. (He was obviously feeling stronger on this occasion than when he tried to carry away church towers in Bedfordshire and Norfolk!) The Vale Royal monks pealed their bells, which so alarmed the Devil that he dropped the church. It was undamaged, and still stands on its fortuitous site.

Stoak church was moved to its present site by the Devil; Ince church was resited by fairies during building.

The site of Winwick church, and the name of the parish, were determined by a pig. Work on the church had been started, but the first night a pig was seen at the site, crying 'We-ee-wick'. He carried the stones one by one to the place where St Oswald, King of Northumbria, was killed in AD 642, and the church founder, seeing this as a sacred sign, recommenced building on the new site. A pig is sculpted on the church tower, just above the west entrance.

Lancashire. The story of the siting of a church at Lady Well, Fernihalgh, north of Preston, bears in one of its features a strong similarity to the stories of Durham and Salisbury cathedrals. A merchant at sea in a gale promised he would perform a pious deed if he survived. He landed safely on the Fylde coast, and a voice told him to build a church 'where a statue of Our Lady stood by a well above which grew a crabtree bearing apples without cores, at a place called Fernihalgh'. Being in unknown territory, the merchant did not know where this place might be, until he overheard a milkmaid telling someone how her cow had strayed to Fernihalgh. Having asked directions, he went there and saw everything as the voice had told him. A new chapel was built in 1796 at a short distance from the spot where there was a small building at least as early as the reign of Henry VI (early fifteenth century), and this earlier building may have been the merchant's church.

Pigs were instrumental in choosing the site of St Peter's church, Burnley, as at Winwick (Cheshire). It was intended to build in Godly Lane where the old Saxon cross now stands, but a number of pigs removed the materials to the church's present site. Again as at Winwick, a pig is sculpted on the church—on the south side of the steeple, and on the old font.

Leyland church should have been sited at Whittle, but during the night following the day when work was completed, the whole building was moved to a new site on a rise at the east of the village. One version credits the removal to a 'supernatural agency', another to a large cat. On the morning following the removal, the villagers found a marble tablet on the church wall with the words:

Here thou shalt be,
And here thou shalt stand,
And thou shalt be called
The church of Ley-land.

In 1511 a church was being built at Newchurch, in Rossendale, and the intended site was at Mitchellfield-nook. But the stones were being removed by night to a new site, so three parishioners kept watch, and were given food and drink by a kind old lady passing by. All fell asleep—and on waking found the stones had been moved again. So the new site was accepted, and the church can still be seen there. The site of Samlesbury church near Preston was also moved.

Greater Manchester. Here is a nineteenth-century rendering of the story of the siting of St Chad's church, Rochdale, from *Lancashire Legends* by J. Harland and T. T. Wilkinson.

Towards the close of the reign of William the Conqueror, Gamel, the Saxon thane, Lord of Recedham or Rochdale, being left in the quiet possession of his lands and privileges, was 'minded, for the fear of God and the salvation of his immortal soul, to build a chapel unto St Chadde', nigh to the banks of the Rache or Roach. According to Mr Roby, in his 'Traditions', a place was set apart on the north bank of the river, in a low and sheltered spot now called 'The Newgate'. Piles of timber and huge stones were gathered in profusion; the foundations were laid; stakes having been driven, and several courses of rubble stone laid ready to receive the grouting or cement. In one night, the whole mass was conveyed, without the loss of a single stone, to the summit of a steep hill on the opposite bank, and apparently without any visible signs of the mode of removal. The Saxon thane was greatly incensed at what he supposed to be a trick of some of his own vassals, and threatened punishment; to obviate which, a number of the villeins and bordarii with great difficulty and labour conveyed the building materials back to the site for the church; but again were they all removed in the night to the top of the hill. Gamel having learned the truth, sought counsel from Holy Church, and it was thereon resolved that the chapel should be built on the hill-top, as the unknown persons would not permit it to be erected on the site originally selected. This explains the chapel or church of St Chadde, still standing on a hill so high that one hundred and twenty-four steps were cut to accomplish the ascent, and enable the good people to go to prayers.

Humberside. Fairies moved the stones of the church at Holme-on-the-Wolds to a new site.

North Yorkshire. The churches of Easingwold, Hinderwell, Leake, Marrick, and North Otterington all have stories of the stones being moved while building was in progress.

Cleveland. Marske church was also resited in this way.

Durham. Monks from Lindisfarne were travelling through the north of England with the body of St Cuthbert when they found they could take it no further—it seemed fixed to the ground. After three days of fasting and praying for guidance it was revealed to them that the saint's body should be carried to Dunholme, there to rest. The location of Dunholme was unknown to them, but shortly afterwards one of the monks overhead a woman talking about her cow which had strayed to that very place. A church was built there, on a cliff above the River Tees, and this later became the site of Durham Cathedral.

Cumbria. A group of monks chose a hilltop site in Cartmel Forest for the church they planned to build, but as they were just about to begin work they heard a voice in the air saying: 'Not there, but in a valley, between two rivers, where the one runs north, and the other south.' Such a site sounded unlikely, but nevertheless the monks searched hard for it. Having been unsuccessful, they were returning to their original site when, in a nearby valley, they found a small river which ran north, and close by another running south. So they built their church of St Mary, Cartmel, on an island between the two.

The site of Crosby Garrett church was moved from the village in the valley to a hilltop. At Arlecdon, a church was being built in Jackson's Park, but at night unknown hands were destroying the work. A watch was kept, but the men claimed to have seen and heard nothing. The workmen took fright and abandoned their work entirely, so that a new site had to be found and the church was built where it now stands.

Church-siting traditions in Wales

Dyfed. St David's church, Llanddewi Brefi (Cardigan), was to have been built in a field at Godregarth Farm, a mile away from the village, but a 'Spirit' pulled down the day's work each night, and carried the stones to the spot where the church now stands.

Penbryn church (Cardigan) should have been built at Penlon Moch, near Sarnau, but the materials were removed 'by invisible hands' to the present church site. There is a similar tradition concerning Bettws Ifan (Cardigan). The parish of Llanfihangel Genau'r Glyn (Llanfihangel = church of Michael) (Cardigan) is about a mile from the farmhouse named Glanfread or Glanfread-fawr, which site was originally intended for the church. But each night the day's work was destroyed, and a voice was heard saying

> Glanfread-fawr sy fod fan hyn,
> Llanfihangel yn Genau'r Glyn.

(Glanfread-fawr is to be herein, Llanfihangel at Genau'r Glyn.) So the church was built at Genau'r Glyn, and a farm at Glanfread-fawr.

The parish church of Llanddeusant (Carmarthen) was to have been built at Twynllanan in the centre of the parish, but by night the stones were removed to the church's present site. Work was slow at the building of Llanwinio church (Carmarthen), for each day's work 'fell down in the night'. The builder threw his hammer into the air (in exasperation, or divination?) and the church was built on the spot where it fell, without further hindrance.

A field called Parc y Fonwent was chosen as the site for Llangan church (Carmarthen), but the stones were carried by night to a new site, accom-

Llanbister church.

panied by a voice saying, 'Llangan, dyma'r fan' (Llangan, here is the spot).

The original site for Maros church (Carmarthen) was a field called Church Park near Pendine, not far west of where the church now stands. By night stones and mortar were removed to the new site by 'invisible spirits'. Also, at Llangeler (Carmarthen), each day's work was carried from the chosen site, at Parc-y-Bwci (Goblin's Park), to the site where the church was finally built.

Powys. The original piece of land chosen for the erection of Llanbister church (Radnor) was close to the spot where the church was actually built. A historian of the county said in 1859 that 'The tradition that a supernatural being carried away in the night whatever was built of the church during the day, is still kept alive, because the warden claims an annual rent of 2s. 6d. for the vacant and unconsecrated site of the originally intended church.' Again we find factual confirmation of a folk tradition.

Clwyd. Wrexham church (Denbigh) was to have been built on low ground at Bryn-y-Hynnon, but the work was disturbed by night, and a voice was heard saying, 'Bryn-y-Grog' (Hill of the Cross), so the church was built there instead. A hilltop site near an ancient spring had been chosen for Capel Garmon church (Denbigh), but it was moved downhill.

Corwen church (Merioneth) was repeatedly demolished during construction until the builders restarted work beside Carreg y Big yn y Fach Rewlyd (the Pointed Stone in the Icy Nook).

Work was started on a church between Cynwyd and Corwen, where Cynwyd Bridge crosses the River Dee. But the stones were removed by the Devil each night. A wise man told the masons that they should build their church where a white stag would first be seen when they were out hunting. They did this, and Llangar church (Merioneth) or the Church of the White Stag (Llan-gaɪw-gwyn) was built on the spot.

Gwynedd. The stones for Llanllechid church near Bangor (Caernarvon) were carried away from a field called Cae'r Capel.

Church-siting traditions in Scotland

Highland. St Erchard (or Merchard) discovered three new bells buried at the foot of a tree in Strathglass (Inverness), having been led to them by a plump white cow, which stood staring at this tree. He gave one each of the bells to his disciples and kept one himself. In a revelation he was told that they must all set out alone, building a church where the bell rang for the third time. Merchard went south, his bell ringing for the first time at the hill Suidh Mhercheird (Merchard's Seat), for the second time at Fuaran Mhercheird (Merchard's Well), Ballintombuie, and for the third time by the River Moriston in Glenmoriston. So he built his church (Clachan Mhercheird) there; the graveyard is all that remains now at Merchard. The other disciples built their churches at Glenconvinth, and at Broadford in Skye.

Grampian. The materials for the church at Firdoun (Kincardine) were moved supernaturally from one site to another.

Sir Walter Scott's Notes to *The Lay of the Last Minstrel* contain details of a siting legend connected with Old Deer church.

When the workmen were engaged in erecting the ancient church of Old Deer, in Aberdeenshire, upon a small hill called Bissau they were surprised to find that the work was impeded by supernatural obstacles. At length the Spirit of the River was heard to say:

> 'It is not here, it is not here,
> That ye shall build the church of Deer;
> But on Taptillery,
> Where many a corpse shall lie.'

The site of the edifice was accordingly transferred to Taptillery, an eminence at some distance from where the building had been commenced.

Western Isles. St Torranan brought Christianity to Benbecula, and decided to build a church on the hillock of Cnoc Feannaig (Knoll of the Hooded Crow) near Cailigeo. He and his helpers worked hard carrying building materials to the site, but every night they were all moved to a small island in a nearby loch. St Torranan blessed the site and sprinkled site and stones with holy water, but it made no difference. So he kept watch, and saw shining angels fly to and fro carrying the stones to the island. He realised that this was a sign to build the church there, and so work was begun on the island. Next day they returned to find the church had been finished overnight, except for the roof, because no materials for this had yet been provided.

These hundred church-siting traditions cover almost every English county, and a number of counties in Scotland and Wales, and they are probably only a small proportion of the traditions that originally existed but that have not been recorded and have faded from folk memory. Similar stories of the overnight moving of stones relate to other buildings too, for example Maudslie Castle (Strathclyde: Lanark), Melgrund Castle (Fife), Callaly Castle (Northumberland), the old mansion of Garnstone (Hereford and Worcester), Buckland Abbey (Devon), and the Devil's Bridge at Kirkby Lonsdale (Cumbria). It is obvious that at one time the siting of buildings was a matter of profound importance and decisions were not made for reasons solely of expediency, as is the case today.

The mass of traditions related here gives support to the ideas outlined earlier in this chapter, that the siting of churches was often subject to disputes between Christians and pagans, and that the sites were often chosen by some form of divination. Presumably the process of mapping the important earth currents and selecting the final site was entrusted to a 'wise man', who retained knowledge of procedures long since lost to most people. His role would be similar to that of the geomancers of China. These practitioners of the ancient art of *feng-shui* guided the Chinese populace, until recent years, not only in the siting of their houses, public buildings, temples and tombs, but also in the planting of shrubs and trees, alterations to the contours of hills and mountains, and the redirection of the flow of streams and rivers. The evidence we present in this book seems to suggest that in the distant past this was also the case in the British Isles (and probably also other parts of the world). But in the era we are at present considering, when Christian churches were being founded and rebuilt, such knowledge in Britain would be the property of a few remaining adepts, and the mass of the populace, not aware of the knowledge and skills which the geomancer was using, could only fabricate fantastic stories to explain a situation that was beyond their comprehension.

The significance of water

One recurrent aspect of these church-siting traditions is the moving of a site from a hilltop to marshy lower ground, or very near water. Cartmel church was built on an island between two streams (which flowed in different directions: this may have had some vital importance in connection with the flow of earth current at the site); Baschurch church was built on a marsh near the river; and there are many other examples, notably several of our finest cathedrals—Salisbury was moved from the high ground of Old Sarum to the low-lying and marshy water-meadows of the Avon; Winchester and Canterbury were built on swamps; Southwark Cathedral and Westminster Abbey were sited on marshy ground by the Thames in London (at one time Westminster Abbey was surrounded by water at high tide); Ely was built on an island in the Fens; Durham, Rochester, and Worcester are close to rivers; St David's is in a hollow and beside a stream; and Hereford, not far from the River Wye, was built on waterlogged ground as the damp in the crypt at the present time indicates. Although it does seem quite senseless to remove a church from a high, and therefore presumably well-drained, site to a lower, wet one, such acts may have been wiser than we of the twentieth century can credit, with our dependence on damp courses and polythene membranes. To the medieval masons and their predecessors, finding the most favourable site for beneficial current flows was probably far more important than the minor discomforts resulting from damp crypts and foundations!

The evidence presented by dowser Guy Underwood in his book *The Pattern of the Past* suggests that water is a highly significant factor in the location of churches. Extensive dowsing surveys showed him that medieval churches were built according to geodetic principles, and that the geodetic lines and blind springs on the chosen site, once located, predetermined to some extent the layout of the church or cathedral. The plans in his book illustrate this. However it has been suggested that Underwood may have

misunderstood the significance of the underground geodetic lines he discovered in the churches where he dowsed: it is possible that the act of
building the church may have affected the lines, causing them to change
course to follow the features of the church, and that they did not in fact
exist in these conformations before the church was built. For example,
he says of Salisbury Cathedral (Wiltshire): 'The spire marks an exception-
ally powerful blind spring in the centre line of the nave, and which has
about eleven branch aquastats and produces six haloes.' We have already
described the 'shape power' theory and the importance of church spires in
bringing down power into the church below (see Chapter One), and the
404-foot spire of Salisbury Cathedral provides a classic example. We would
expect it to have the powerful effect discovered by Underwood; but whereas he believed the spire was erected to mark the significant geodetic features,
we believe that the effect of the spire is so strong that the power it concentrates into the cathedral has an effect on the ground beneath. The same
argument can be applied to the ancient sites Underwood dowsed, such as
Stonehenge, stone circles, and hill figures. Here the same connection between the shape of the sites' features and the geodetic lines can be clearly
seen in his illustrations. Whichever existed first, the geodetic lines or the
surface structures, Underwood's discoveries are still valid, and help to
show how pervasive are the influences of the earth currents and how closely
related they are to the shape of the earth's surface and the structures upon
it.

6 Restless stones and ancient rituals

The Nine Maidens on Belstone Common, which are said to dance daily at noon.

Some of the ancient standing stones were difficult to move (as will be described in Chapter Eight), and anyone who tried to move them had a hard task, even though several strong horses and heavy chains were used. But there were other stones which were said to move of their own accord, without any human aid, to turn round, dance, drink, and generally behave as if alive, and an examination of the traditions which tell why and when they performed these activities may increase our insight into the workings of the earth currents.

Stones on the move

The Dancing Stones of Stackpole (Dyfed: Pembroke) are three standing stones about one mile apart: Sampson Cross, Harold's Stone, and another

Every night the Four Stones near Old Radnor (Powys: Radnor) used to go down to the Hindwell Pool to drink.

at Stackpole Warren. Sometimes they get together and go down to Saxon's (or Sais's) Ford to dance the hay (a country-dance), and any witnesses are assured of good luck. Other dancing stones include the Waterstone at Wrington (Avon) (which dances when there is a full moon on Midsummer's Day), the Nine Stones or Nine Maidens on Belstone Common (Devon) (which move or dance daily at noon), and the Wimblestone near Shipham (Somerset) (one tale tells how a countryman saw this twelve-foot stone dancing in the moonlight, which shone on a heap of gold lying where the stone usually stood).

On Midsummer Eve, the stones of St Lythans chambered cairn near St Nicholas (South Glamorgan) whirl around three times and curtsey. The stones of the Grey Wethers stone circle on Sittaford Tor, Dartmoor (Devon), go for a short walk at sunrise, while the Longstone, above

The Wergin Stone stands almost forgotten in a field north of Hereford.

Chagford (Devon), turns round slowly at sunrise in order to warm each side in turn. The Giant's Stone at Yetnasteen on Rousay (Orkney) walks each New Year's morning to the Loch of Scockness for a drink; also in Orkney, and at the very same time, the Stane o' Quoybune, on Birsay, goes down to a loch to drink. Both stones must be back before dawn, and tradition tells how a sailor who sat up to watch the Stane o' Quoybune was crushed to death by it when he got in its way. In County Wicklow, the Motty Stone on Cronebane Hill (south of Rathdrum) goes to wash at the Upper Meeting of the Waters once a year on May Day morning.

Two stories of stones which moved mysteriously only on one occasion and in recent centuries come from the Highlands and Hereford and Worcester. The Wergin Stone, Sutton, near Hereford was moved 240 paces from its former position some time in 1652, no one knew how, and it needed nine yoke of oxen to take it back. In the Highlands (Inverness) the Stone of Petti, which weighed approximately eight tons and formerly marked part of the boundary between Culloden estate and Moray county about 500 yards inland, was mysteriously transported 260 yards out to sea during the stormy night of 20 February 1799. This event is said to have been foretold by the Brahan Seer, who said, 'No one will see it removed or be able to account for its sudden and marvellous transportation.'

A prediction of the stone's displacement was also credited to another Highland seer, Reverend John Morrison. During one of his sermons he is said to have exclaimed: 'Ye sinful and stiff-necked people, God will, unless ye turn from your evil ways, sweep you ere long into the place of torment; and, as a sign of the truth of what I say, Clach Dubh an Abhainn, large though it be, will be carried soon, without human agency, a considerable distance seawards.' His prediction was rather premature, however, because the stone was not moved until twenty-six years later!

As mentioned at the beginning of this chapter, several human characteristics have been attributed to stones: movement, dancing, drinking, washing (all illustrated above), eating and drinking (illustrated by the stories of libations of milk and offerings of food left on stones which we described in Chapter Two), and the possible sexual associations suggested by the shapes of some stones (also discussed in Chapter Two). It has been proposed elsewhere (for example, in T. F. G. Dexter's *The Sacred Stone*) that such stories indicate a belief that stones were alive, and such a belief may indeed have existed. Evidence to support it comes from the parish register of St Mary's church, Reading (Berkshire) where a notice dated 26 July 1602 reads: 'This child was killed by a blocke which fell upon him; which blocke was founde by the Corowner's Jury to be guilty of his death.' Further evidence may lie in the belief, which was especially strong in East Anglia, that stones grew. The Blaxhall Stone at Stone Farm, Blaxhall (Suffolk) is said to have grown from the size of a small loaf a century ago to its present weight of about five tons; in 1893 a Suffolk farmer declared that stones grew in the earth, so there was no point in clearing them off the land—a belief formerly widely held; and another Suffolk man, living in Martlesham, kept on his windowsill a conglomeration of pebbles (pudding-stone) which he called a mother stone, because he thought it was the parent of the pebbles that formed it. A clergyman who was trying to convince a man that stones did not grow said: 'But if you put a stone on that mantelpiece, and look at it in five years, you will find that it has not grown.' To which the reply was: 'Noa, and I hreckon if you put a 'tater there, it would not grow, either.' The man made his point: that nothing will grow if the conditions are not right. And who are we to reject out of hand his belief in the ability of stones to grow? They are not inert lumps, but groups of atoms and molecules just as we are, and maybe stones continually renew their parts, as our bodies do. It is more likely, however, that this belief in growing stones is all that remains of an ancient knowledge of the earth currents and their effects on stones.

In fact it may well be that all the beliefs relating to stones moving could be the degenerate remnants of earlier knowledge of the true significance of standing stones. Clues that this may be so can be found in the many stories of stones turning when the cock crows or when the clock strikes twelve.

These two features recur frequently, as the following examples show. The Cock-Crow Stone at Wellington (Somerset) turns round every time the cock crows, and this is when you might be able to see the treasure lying beneath the stone. Another Cock-Crow Stone was at Looe, Cornwall (now beneath the water of Looe harbour), and this turned round three times whenever it heard a cock crow in the nearby farmyard of Hay. There are also 'cock-crowing' stones near Sheffield (South Yorkshire) (for example, the Cock-Crowing Stone or Stump John, at Hollow Meadows, which turns round on one morning—not specified—each year when the cock crows) and near Ashover (Derbyshire). The topmost stone of the Cheesewring (Cornwall) turns round three times when it hears the cock crow, while the stone marking the Giant's Grave at Melcombe Horsey (Dorset) moves when it hears the cocks crowing in nearby Chesilborne, and the Whetstone on Hergest Ridge, Kington (Hereford and Worcester) goes down to drink every morning, when it hears the cock crow. Other stones which turn round when they hear the cock crow are the Eagle Stone at Curbar (Derbyshire), a large boulder near Great Huglith (Salop), and the Whirlstone, a stone weighing several tons which stands in the middle of a brook near The Beach, Marton (Salop).

Someone wrote a rhyme about the Bulmer Stone in Northgate Street, Darlington (Durham), a granite boulder which stood (and may still stand) in front of the cottages known as Northgate House.

> In Darntoun Towne there is a stane,
> And most strange yt is to tell,
> That yt turnes IX times round aboute,
> When yt hears ye clock strike twell.

And another verse encapsulates a tradition concerning the Ham Stone at Stoke-sub-Hamdon (Somerset):

> When Ham Stone hears the Norton chimes at midnight clack,
> It rolls down hill to drink at Jack O' Beards and back.

The Wych Boulder at Wych (Lincolnshire) turns over when the clock strikes twelve, and the Colwall Stone (Hereford and Worcester) turns round completely when the clock strikes midnight. The Tingle Stone at the long barrow near Avening (Gloucestershire) runs round the field when it

Opposite: This impressive rock formation on Bodmin Moor is known as the Cheesewring, and its topmost stone is said to turn round three times when it hears the cock crow. Perhaps it is fortunate that farmyards are few and far between on the desolate moorland which surrounds it.

Left: When Moreton church clock chimes midnight, this wayside cross, known as Stumpy Cross and still to be seen at a crossroads between Moreton Hampstead and North Bovey (Devon), is said to revolve slowly three times.

Right: The Pyrford Stone.

hears the clock strike midnight, and another Gloucestershire stone, the Long Stone at Minchinhampton, runs (or walks) round the field when the clock strikes twelve. The Whittlestone near Lower Swell (Gloucestershire) used to go down and drink from the Lady Well when the clock struck twelve, and an old cross shaft at East Catkill Farm, south of Rose Ash on the Devon side of Exmoor, turns round when it hears the clock strike (but no time is specified). The Lea Stone in a field at Lea in Salop is said to turn round when the clock strikes thirteen. Whether a mistake occurred at some time when the details of this tradition were being copied, or whether thirteen was used to emphasise the impossibility of the event, is open to all to decide for themselves. The story relating to the Pyrford Stone in Surrey combines both cock-crow and clock-strike features, and tells how the stone turns when it hears the cock crow at dawn, and also when the clock on nearby St Nicholas's church strikes midnight. The church has never had a clock, and this fact indicates that some at least of these stories may be regarded as jokes. A number of them stress the point that the stone moves when it *hears* the clock strike, or when it *hears* the cock crow— everyone knows of course that stones cannot hear, and therefore that they could move is equally impossible. This aspect of these stories is probably a relatively late development, which took place when the earlier belief in stones having life became unacceptable and some new explanation was needed for the familiar traditions which embodied this belief.

These traditions are significant in that a specific time is usually mentioned, particularly when the clock strikes twelve or midnight, also cock-crow, i.e. dawn, but certain days of the year are sometimes specified: Midsummer Eve, at full moon on Midsummer Day, New Year's morning, May Day morning. Would this be the case if all these traditions were jokes? Times are also stipulated in other traditions not concerned with stones turning, for example, anyone touching the Witches' Rock near Zennor (Cornwall) nine times at midnight was insured against bad luck; and also in Cornwall, there was a logan rock at Nancledra near St Ives which could only be moved at midnight. To effect a cure for rickets, children had to be placed on the rock at that time. In Chapter Two are a number of accounts of the healing and fertilising powers of stones which can be tapped by performing a ritual at a specific time, for example during May, at midnight, before sunrise. One explanation for this feature is that the time stated is the time when the current in the stone is at its most favourable, and therefore most likely to help bring about the desired result. This does not apply, however, to the traditions of a stone moving or turning at midnight, cock-crow, etc. In these cases, the 'turning' of the stone may indicate that the time specified is a time of polarity change—the turning of the current. The times specified are themselves turning points: midnight, when one day ends and another begins; twelve, which (if twelve noon is meant) is the day's midpoint; and cock-crow or dawn, the end of darkness and coming of daylight. Turning points in the year are sometimes mentioned, such as May Day and Midsummer. That the full moon must fall on Midsummer's Day before the Waterstone at Wrington (Avon) will dance, indicates that there may sometimes be cosmic influences on the currents passing through the stones.

Nine times round

Not only is it important to perform a ritual at a certain time, but in some cases it is also vital that the ritual be performed the correct number of times. This usually applies to those rituals which involve walking or running round a stone or site, and the number of times this must be done is very often three or a multiple of three, usually nine. At Tullybelton in Strathtay (Tayside: Perth) a well was visited on Beltane morning (1 May) and after drinking there, the visitors had to walk round it nine times in a clockwise direction, and then round the standing stones beside it. Youngsters wishing at the Wishing Post, a stone in the dungeon of Oystermouth Castle (West Glamorgan), had to walk round it nine times as part of the ritual, and girls following the ritual at St Patrick's Well on the Isle of Man

This old drawing depicts the ritual which used to be performed round the Funeral Stone at Brilley. The stone can be seen as a squat block round which the mourners are walking, following in the wake of the coffin bearers.

(described in Chapter Two) had to walk three times sunwise round the White Lady of Ballafreer, a white quartz pillar standing close by the well. At Sennen in Cornwall, the old folk used to go nine times daily round the Garrack Zans (or Table Mên), a large flat stone, because to do so brought good luck and protection against witchcraft. There was once a rocking stone called Cryd Tudno (Tudno's Cradle) on Great Orme's Head (Gwynedd: Caernarvon), and mothers who wanted to help their children to learn to walk would every week get them to crawl three times round the stone. Also in Wales, girls would crawl three times round Arthur's Stone, in Gower (West Glamorgan), in order to test their sweethearts' fidelity. (This ritual is described more fully in Chapter Two.) On Knightlow Hill near Ryton-on-Dunsmore (Warwickshire) it is still the custom for the representatives of twenty-five parishes making up the Hundred of Knightlow to meet by Knightlow Cross at sunrise on 11 November every year to pay the Wroth Silver to the agent of the Duke of Buccleuch. The remains of the old wayside cross stand on top of a tumulus, and it was originally the custom for all present to walk three times round the stone before the proceedings began. The Stone of Odin, Stenness (Orkney) was, until its destruction in 1814, highly venerated, and a farmer who wished for magical powers visited it at the full moon in nine consecutive months. On each occasion, he went round the stone on bare knees nine times, and then made his wish while looking through the hole in the stone.

The importance of going round a stone sunwise is often mentioned, and presumably to go round in the opposite direction would either produce no result, or the opposite to that intended. Sir Walter Scott recorded that people believed it to be unlucky to ride widdershins, i.e. opposite to sunwise, three times round the Keeldar Stone (in Northumberland, on the English/Scottish border, probably the same stone as is marked 'Kielder Stone' on modern maps).

At funerals, coffins were sometimes carried round churchyard crosses or even older stones, and one example of this, at Manaton in Devon, has already been described in Chapter Five. There the procession was sunwise, and three times round the cross. In the case of the Funeral Stone just outside the churchyard at Brilley (Hereford and Worcester), no direction

The iron railings take much of the atmosphere away from Kit's Coty House, the three upright stones topped by a capstone being all that remains of a Neolithic burial chamber.

is specified, but the coffin was carried three times round the stone (which no longer exists), in order to prevent the Devil from taking the dead person's soul. In the corner of St Luke's churchyard at Formby (Merseyside) is the Godstone, round which a corpse was thrice carried so that the spirit of the departed would not return to haunt the relatives. The original intention may have been to use the current flowing through or from the stone to break any remaining ties with the earth, and help release the spirit and aid its journey to the next realm of existence, but it probably later degenerated into an empty ritual.

There are of course exceptions to the ritual of going nine or three times round a site. A block of stone called the Stone of the Swan (Clach na-h-ealea) in a field opposite the old cathedral on the island of Lismore (Strathclyde: Argyll) could give sanctuary to anyone who ran round it sunwise (the number of times is not specified, so presumably once was enough), or simply seized hold of it. The 'Elders' considered the case of anyone claiming sanctuary in this way, and if they decided in favour of the claimant, they walked sunwise round the stone. If their decision was a negative one, however, they walked round anti-clockwise and handed the claimant over to 'Authority' for trial.

The following variation sounds rather pointless, for nothing positive is achieved. Only a criminal wishing to get rid of an incriminating artefact is likely to find this ritual useful! It involves placing a personal object on the capstone of the dolmen Kit's Coty House in Kent, and then walking round the stones three times, at which the object will disappear. This ritual must be performed at full moon, and it has been suggested that it is all that remains of a sacrificial ritual. A similar tradition comes from Westleton in Suffolk, where a large stone (sometimes called the Witch's Stone) lies hidden in the grass by the chancel door of St Peter's church. Children used to put a handkerchief or a straw in the wall grating above the stone, and then run round the church three (or seven) times. Afterwards, they looked at the grating and saw that the object had disappeared (or the rattling of chains was heard).

This conventionally eerie sound leads us to the next group of traditions, as also does the mention of the number seven. It would seem that this number and potentially unpleasant events go together, for here are two traditions which tell of running seven times round a site in order to conjure up the Devil. This is told of Cymbeline's Castle, an earthwork in Chequers Park, Great Kimble (Buckinghamshire), and also of the hillfort on Chanctonbury Ring (West Sussex), although in this case it is necessary to run backwards seven times round the clump of trees on the summit of the hill,

Opposite: The beech trees on top of Chanctonbury Ring were planted within the area of the hillfort in 1760.

at midnight on Midsummer Eve. Anyone successfully completing this arduous feat (for the clump of trees is not small) can expect to see the Devil, who appears bearing a bowl of porridge, in exchange for which he will take your soul. (There must be easier ways of getting a bowl of porridge!) If, having accepted and eaten the Devil's porridge, you feel fit for more adventures, an accurate counting of the trees on the Ring (generally reckoned to be uncountable) will provide an even more impressive result than a porridge-bearing Devil: the raising of the ghosts of Julius Caesar and his armies.

There are other places where the Devil can be summoned, such as Bungay in Suffolk. To run twelve times round the three-foot high Druid's Stone near the porch of St Mary's Priory church after calling upon the Devil would be sure to bring him out; and in Lincolnshire, the Bound Stone in Spring Hills at Hemswell was visited by children who pricked it with pins (into the natural hollows on its surface), ran round it very fast several times, and then put their ears close to it, whereupon they could, by listening hard, hear the Devil speak.

It is extremely interesting that the numbers three (and multiples thereof) and seven feature so prominently in this section, because these are the same two numbers Guy Underwood found to be so important when he was investigating the underground geodetic features at ancient sites. Of the three main types of geodetic line he says:

The water line, the aquastat and the track line have much in common: they appear to be generated within the Earth; to involve wave-motion; to have great penetrative power; to form a network on the face of the Earth; to affect the germination and manner of growth of certain trees and plants; to be perceived and used by animals; to affect opposite sides of the animal body, and to form spiral patterns. They are controlled by mathematical laws which involve in their construction the number 3; and in their spiral patterns, the number 7. They played a prominent, and possibly fundamental, part in the religion of many widely scattered primitive peoples. (*The Pattern of the Past*)

It is surely not coincidence that the rituals described in this section often involve running round a site three or seven times, while the features Underwood associates with these same numbers, but especially seven, take the form of coiled spirals. It was not until we had collected and arranged the material in this section that Underwood's findings came to our notice, so it cannot be claimed that we were influenced by them. Further confirmation of the apparent significance of three and seven can be found in Chapter Three, in the quotation from Harland and Wilkinson relating to the allegorical nature of dragon traditions, and these same numbers also recur again and again throughout this book.

Although the outcome of the rituals in this section varies, the procedure is always the same, and necessitates running round a site, usually a single standing stone. One explanation of this action might be that it is all that remains of a more complex ritual performed in order to 'raise the power'—rather in the same way that witches used to dance at stone circles as described in Chapter One. Fast running round a stone will make the runner feel dizzy, and might loosen the astral body, facilitating communication with other levels. The results of the rituals as reported today—conjuring up the Devil, causing objects to disappear, bringing good luck, etc.—are simply much-distorted memories of the benefits (or dangers) resulting from the correct manipulation of (or injudicious tampering with) the earth currents.

An assortment of rituals

While talking about degenerate rituals it is appropriate to introduce a number of traditions which are difficult to categorise and which, in our researches at least, have not been duplicated. Their interpretation, also, is often not easy, but we felt they should be included nevertheless, because they are traditions relating to ancient sites, and because their themes do carry familiar overtones.

First, a tradition from Shebbear in Devon, where the Devil's Stone is turned over every year on the evening of 5 November. The stone is just outside the churchyard, and the ceremony, performed by the church bell-ringers using crowbars, takes place preceded and followed by bell-ringing, which is intended to frighten away the Devil. If the stone were not turned, it would mean bad luck for the village. The Devil is said to lie beneath the stone, and the ritual turning ensures that he stays there for another year, which rather contradicts the purpose of the earlier bell-ringing. This seems to be yet another example of a ritual distorted by centuries, maybe even thousands of years, of incomprehension of what was actually being done. If we substitute 'earth currents' for 'Devil', it becomes clearer that the ritual may have originally been intended to avert the disaster which could be brought about by a build-up of energy in the stone, and therefore the 'pressure' needed to be released annually by the turning of the stone. If this were not done, the accumulated energy would cause a local catastrophe of a similar nature to those to be described in Chapter Eight, which were also due to the mishandling of earth currents. Today, of course, it is doubtful if any harm would be caused were the Devil's Stone to be left unturned. The power network has been neglected for so long that its strength is now generally weak. However, no one can really know the

The Devil's Stone at Shebbear.

condition of that part of the circuit which passes through the Devil's Stone in Shebbear, and perhaps the villagers are wise to maintain what is probably a millennia-old custom.

Two stones with unusual stories can be found about a mile from the Green Gorge on Penmaenmawr (Gwynedd: Caernarvon). The story of the Deity Stone, which would bend its head and hit anyone blaspheming in its presence, is told here by Marie Trevelyan in *Folk-Lore and Folk-Stories of Wales*.

A man from South Wales played cards with some friends beside this stone on a Sunday, and when the men returned to the village with cuts about their heads, the people knew the Deity Stone had smitten them, though they would not admit having had punishment. A notorious blasphemer who came from Merionethshire laughed to scorn the story of this stone. One night he went to the Druids' Circle alone and at a very late hour, and shouted words of blasphemy so loud that his voice could be heard ringing down the Green Gorge. People shuddered as they heard him. The sounds ceased, and the listeners ran away in sheer fright. In the morning the blasphemer's corpse was found in a terribly battered condition at the base of the Deity Stone.

Opposite the Deity Stone is the Stone of Sacrifice, which has a depression on top large enough to hold a baby. It was believed that good luck could be obtained for any baby placed there for a few minutes before it was one month old. This belief is in line with the many healing and fertility traditions described in Chapter Two; the power in the stone is transferred to the baby by physical contact. The power could also be used against witches, it was believed, for it was a custom to sprinkle rainwater from the depression on to the threshold, as a protection against them. The stone's power to subdue witches went even further, however. A group of them held a revel at the stones one day, and when the ritual was at its height 'stern maledictions' were heard coming from the stone, which so frightened the witches that two died suddenly and one went mad. It is a possibility that the witches' dancing caused an accumulation of energy beyond the danger point, and that the resulting discharge caused them physical and mental injury. They obviously did not appreciate the magnitude of the power with which they were tampering.

A giant lived near Kinveachy (Highland: Inverness) and, so the tradition goes, he removed his heart and hid it in the Bonnet Stone in Kinveachy Woods, in order to stop people killing him. The only way to kill him was for a man to lay his bonnet on the stone while the heart was in it, whereupon it would die. If the giant saw a man wearing a bonnet anywhere near the stone, he would quickly take his heart and hide it in a different stone. The meaning behind this curious story is obscure, but the 'giant's heart in a stone' could be one way of saying that the stone too had life, i.e. the earth current which flowed through it. The giant's custom of moving the heart from stone to stone could symbolise the variability of current within any individual stone; and the killing of the heart could be equated with the draining of current from a stone by human beings. The importance of a man's bonnet to the operation could indicate that the 'priests' who were entrusted with the handling of the stones and the manipulation of the currents wore special hats, possibly the same shape as the traditional dunce's cap, which is a tall cone. Church spires are also this shape, and, as suggested in Chapter One, it may be that it has an importance beyond the purely aesthetic. The study of 'shape power' suggests that the elongated cone of the spire is important in drawing down cosmic power into the church, and the dunce's cap may originally have had a similar function—to attract extra mental energy into the dull-witted scholar. Witches and wizards have also been pictured wearing hats of a similar shape, and they too were involved in power manipulations.

Brahan Wood, near Dingwall (Highland: Ross and Cromarty) also concealed an unusual stone, the Gara Howl (garadh tholl), which was a dolmen-like holed rock. This was used in divination ceremonies, and one story tells of a man from the Loch Ness area who was advised to visit

Gara Howl. He sat beside it for a long time, but no answer was forthcoming to his question. Suddenly, however, he heard a bird calling 'Go to Epack—go to Epack!' They told him in a neighbouring village that a wise woman of that name lived on the Mulbuie in the Black Isle. So he visited her, and she answered his question. This could be a case of tuning in to higher forces as a result of a period of meditation at a power source. Perhaps the man's psychic abilities became keener, and the guidance 'Go to Epack' came to him from his subconscious, the words exteriorising in the form of a bird call, in other words an aural hallucination.

Much simpler is the procedure necessary at the Heaven Stone in Trumpan churchyard on the Isle of Skye. The visitor must try to place his finger in a hole in the stone, keeping his eyes shut. If he succeeds, he knows that he will go to Heaven; if he fails, he is headed in the opposite direction. This practice involves making contact with the stone in order to tap its power, but the Heaven/Hell prediction is somewhat ridiculous; one explanation is that it is a degeneration of the belief that if you make contact with the stone you benefit by an intake of the revivifying current (i.e. go to Heaven), and if you don't make contact you do not receive this benefit.

In Farranglogh townland (Meath) are two pillar-stones called the Speaking Stones which were said actually to speak the answers to questions asked of them. They were used to break fairy spells, to cure the effects of the evil eye, and to trace thieves and evil-doers. They could also tell where lost or stolen property was hidden. However, they are now silent because a condition of use was broken: they were asked the same question twice, which was forbidden. One interpretation of this tradition is that a visit to the stones and the resulting power intake helped the supplicant to make use of his own dormant psychic powers. The voice he heard came from his subconscious, which also supplied the answer to his question.

The pillar-stone of Cnamchoill, near Tipperary, and a mass of rock near Rath Coole (Dublin) are said to be all that remains of a flying wheel manufactured by Mog Ruith, Arch-Druid of Erin, and Simon Magus. The wheel, known as Roth Fáil or Roth Rámhach, was used by Simon in Italy to demonstrate his superior magical powers, so the story goes, but it crashed, seriously injuring him. Mog Ruith's daughter Tlachtga took the fragments back to Ireland and positioned them as stated above. It was said that anyone looking at the stones would go blind, and instant death was the fate of anyone touching them. This warning indicates that the stones, whatever their original use (the 'flying wheel' story is probably an allegory concealing an ancient ability—the power to levitate?), were at one time highly charged with the mysterious cosmic energy and that to interfere with them in any way was fraught with physical danger.

The significance of quartz

It would be a long and arduous task to determine the geological composition of the many standing stones described in this book, and even more difficult to ascertain whether the rock was local, or from how far away it was brought. But there are instances where it is known that stones have been moved a considerable distance, and this suggests that the practice may have been more widespread than is realised. Two instances of which we know are the bluestones at Stonehenge, and the Rudston monolith. The first were imported possibly from as far away as Wales, and the Rudston monolith (Humberside) is a block of gritstone whose nearest source seems to be at least ten miles away. Such stones must have been needed for a specific purpose, otherwise the builders could have used local stone. The labour involved in transporting large blocks of stone across rough country and areas of water must have been considerable, and therefore it must have been of the greatest importance that the correct type of stone with its own individual properties was obtained. It has been suggested that the megalith builders may have known how to counteract gravity and negate a stone's weight. Though this possibility should not be wholly dismissed, and it could in fact help to explain the enigmatic megalithic constructions that exist as ruins worldwide, we cannot assume that early man had this ability, in view of the lack of positive evidence. The story of giants Cormoran and Cormelian who built St Michael's Mount in Cornwall (given in full in Chapter Four) describes how Cormoran insisted on bringing white granite from some distance, rather than using a nearer supply of greenstone. Our knowledge of geology is slight, but might 'white granite' be a way of describing granitic stone with a high percentage of quartz?

Quartz is often to be seen at ancient sites, by design rather than by accident we feel, and its importance to the megalith builders is further emphasised in a number of folklore traditions and archaeological discoveries. Three good examples of large quartz stones at ancient sites are the White Lady of Ballafreer on the Isle of Man, a white quartz pillar six to seven feet high (the rituals associated with it are described earlier in this chapter, and also in Chapter Two); the granite stone circle of Boscawen-un, St Buryan (Cornwall), one of the stones of which is a large block of white quartz about four feet high; and the piece of white quartz beside the holed stone at Glencolumbkill (Donegal), where women went to pray for children. Pieces of quartz have been found with prehistoric burials, as in a tumulus at Carrowmore (Sligo) where a cremated burial was accompanied by white quartz pebbles, which are not naturally found in that district, and in a cist at Barnasraghy in the same county, which was filled with pieces of angular-shaped white quartz. In a cairn at Achnacree near Loch

This overgrown circle with a leaning centre stone is the Boscawen-un stone circle, known as the Nine Maidens and traditionally said to be girls turned to stone for dancing on the Sabbath. The stone in the centre foreground is the block of quartz referred to in the text.

Etive (Strathclyde: Argyll), a row of quartz pebbles was found lying on a granite ledge, and shield-shaped pieces of quartz were discovered in the Celtic cemetery at Harlyn Bay (Cornwall). There are other examples, and also many more where white pebbles, not specifically quartz, are mentioned. Were these perhaps a substitute, used when quartz stones were unobtainable or the real significance of quartz forgotten? Such customs die hard. Until recently, crystals of quartz and white stones (called Godstones) were placed in Irish graves; and the fisherfolk of Inveraray (Strathclyde: Argyll) followed the custom of placing white pebbles on the graves of their friends. The importance of white stones at burial sites is echoed in an old custom still practised in 1804 in Glamorgan, where gravestones were whitened with lime at Easter, Whitsuntide, and Christmas.

Quartz, a crystalline mineral, has many interesting qualities. Notable are its piezo-electric properties, which means that it can produce an electric current when put under tension or pressure. When it is influenced by an electric field it will vibrate rapidly at frequencies measured in millions per second and is therefore used in resonators and oscillators for frequency control in electronic communications equipment. It is not an uncommon mineral and granite will usually contain between twenty and forty per cent quartz. Many if not all standing stones and circles must contain a large amount of this substance.

Offerings of white or quartz stones were made at holy wells, such as Ffynnon Degla (Clwyd: Denbigh) and Ffynnon Gwenfaen on Anglesey (Gwynedd), and in both Wales and Scotland charms of quartz and rock crystals were used to give the water of healing wells a magical potency. Although this practice at first glance appears to be mere superstition, it could well be soundly based. If quartz and other minerals have vibratory potencies that can restore a natural harmony to tissues and cells that are diseased, then using pure well water as a medium for conveying the healing properties makes good sense. Similarly in modern medical practice a substance of natural origin is isolated, concentrated, and ingested by the patient as a liquid medicine or a pill taken with water.

W. G. Wood-Martin has collected together in his *Traces of the Elder Faiths of Ireland* several folk beliefs relating to quartz. None of them originates in the British Isles, but that does not invalidate them. In fact it emphasises one aspect of our theme that we have no space to illustrate fully: that all the folklore of ancient sites described in this book is by no means peculiar to the British Isles, but is repeated in many parts of the world, even the remotest areas. The first of Wood-Martin's quartz-related beliefs concerns the Australian aborigines, who considered the possession of crystal vital to the successful work of their medicine man. The Apache Indians of America regarded quartz crystals as 'good medicine', and the Tasmanians, a race now extinct, 'believed that stones, especially certain kinds of quartz crystals, could be used as mediums, or as means of communication with spirits, with the dead, or with living persons at a distance'. The rain-maker of the Australian aboriginal Ta-Ta-thi tribe uses quartz crystal in his rituals, according to J. G. Frazer in *The Golden Bough*, and Mircea Eliade records that aboriginal medicine-men are sprinkled with liquefied quartz at their initiations, which enables them to see the dead and ascend into heaven, and also confers clairvoyant abilities.

This widespread use of quartz, its electrical characteristics, and its frequent association with the dead suggest that it has unusual properties for high frequency communication which, though unknown to the technicians of today, were known and used by early peoples who were able thus to communicate with each other at a distance, and with other levels of existence. But such ideas are anathema to the Establishment. Left, as we are now, with a few crumbling stones and some distorted traditions, obsessed by materialism and having a complete disregard for the natural harmonies of this planet, how can we ever hope to become aware of the thoughts and attitudes of the men of prehistory?

7 Fairies, witches, ghosts, and UFOs

Fairies frolicking, and luring the unsuspecting moorland wanderer into their strange world ... Witches revelling in midnight orgies at stone circles ... Ghosts adding an eeriness to already atmosphere-laden ancient sites ... UFOs secretly visiting remote relics of our past ... Undoubtedly all are attracted to the prehistoric focal points and we must include them in our study, but we will only concern ourselves with their interaction with the ancient sites, because many books have been written on the wider aspects of all four subjects, and there is no space here to enlarge on such things as the fairies' frequent abduction of mortals, their substitution of changelings for human babies, and their unwanted interference in the lives of ordinary people; or the incredible witch-mania that attacked Europe in the Middle Ages, resulting in millions tortured and killed; or the many arguments and theories which have been published concerning the nature and provenance of both ghosts and UFOs.

Fairies

For readers unfamiliar with traditional fairy lore we should emphasise that today's conventional image of a fairy as a pretty diaphanous creature with gossamer wings fluttering among the dewy flowers owes more to fiction than to reported fact. There may be certain 'elementals' which appear in this form, but fairies, or the 'Little People', belong to a different class altogether. They were called the Little People because this term described them: they were, as far as the human eye could judge, normally formed people but small in stature. Their dress, too, often set them apart from ordinary mortals and made them conspicuous. Some of their other characteristics will become apparent from what follows.

Although fairy beliefs have persisted longest in those areas furthest from the effects of civilisation—Wales, Scotland, and Ireland (especially the west)—there are fairy traditions in most parts of the British Isles, and it is true to say that the belief in fairies is by no means dead. The Little People are still seen from time to time. Who they are and where they come from are difficult questions to answer, and a number of possibilities have been proposed, including the following:

1. That they were the remnants of a race formerly inhabiting the British Isles, perhaps of pigmy stature. As 'civilisation' advanced, they were gradually forced further into the wilds where they lived in houses covered with earth and turf. From this may have arisen the belief in the existence of fairy mounds. They kept away from the other inhabitants of the land and so were considered a mysterious race. (Details of people in the British Isles who still lived in earth houses in the last century can be found in

From an old English chapbook comes this woodcut of fairies dancing. On the left is a fairy hill, probably a tumulus; and in the tree can be seen the face of a Green Man, similar to the church carving illustrated in Chapter Five. The object in the foreground may be a stylised toadstool, but in certain respects it also resembles a UFO.

Arthur Mitchell's fascinating book *The Past in the Present*.)
2. That they were witches (or, in even earlier times, the followers of the pre-Christian pagan religion). That is, a group of people with a secret way of life, generally regarded with suspicion by outsiders.
3. That they were a race memory of the Druids and their magical practices.
4. That they were a race memory of the old pagan gods of the early Celts.
5. That they were the spirits of the dead.
6. That they are nature spirits.
7. That they are psychic manifestations.
8. That they are the occupants of UFOs.

The association of the fairies with ancient sites, especially earthworks, is a strong one, particularly in Ireland, where they were often thought to live in the so-called fairy-forts. This formula for visiting the fairies is quoted from *Traces of the Elder Faiths of Ireland* by W. G. Wood-Martin.

If you walk nine times round a fairy rath [an earthen ring-fort] at the full of the moon, the entrance into the underground fairy mansion will become visible, but if the adventurer enters he must abstain from eating, drinking, or kissing a young fairy wench; if he does [any of these] he will never be able to return to earth, or leave the enchanted palace.

Willy Howe is a Neolithic round barrow 24 feet high and 130 feet across, one of the largest in Britain.

The need to walk round the rath nine times is significant, as we have already stressed in Chapter Six. Presumably the completion of this ritual caused the expansion of consciousness which was necessary before the visitor could see the fairies. Often, it seems, those who did visit the fairies were unable to resist the temptations, and suffered accordingly, but a tale from Humberside, recorded by twelfth-century chronicler William of Newburgh, tells how a bold young man outwitted his hosts. A mound near Wold Newton called Willy Howe was said to be inhabited by the fairies. Late one night, after an evening's drinking, the young man was passing Willy Howe on his return home when he heard sounds of merry-making. Riding close to the mound, he saw a door in its side, and through it could be seen a large room full of men and women feasting. One of them brought him a cup to drink from but, knowing that if he did so he would lose consciousness and be carried inside, he poured out the contents and galloped off with the cup. The fairies were unable to catch him, and so he had a cup of an unknown material as a souvenir of his strange encounter.

Pudding Pie Hill near Thirsk in North Yorkshire was also a dwelling place of the fairies, while the Hill of Ile on Islay (Strathclyde: Argyll) was thought to be the home of the Fairy Queen herself. Hob Hurst's House, a round barrow at Beeley (Derbyshire), was the home of Hob Hurst, a goblin, and there are throughout the British Isles many barrows whose names include the word 'fairy': for example, the Fairy's Cradle at Hetton (Durham), the Fairy Toot near Batcombe (Somerset), and the

Below: Overlooking Bassenthwaite Lake, Castle Howe hillfort is said once to have been a fairy haunt.

Overleaf: Legend has it that the hillfort known as South Cadbury Castle (Somerset), which archaeological excavation has shown was occupied from before 3300 BC to late Saxon times, was King Arthur's Camelot.

Fairy Toot at Stoney Littleton (Avon). There were several fairy haunts in West Sussex—Harrow Hill near Patching, where the flint mines and earthworks were said to be the last home of fairies in England; Pulborough Mount, where a fairy funeral was seen; Cissbury Ring, a spacious hilltop fort where the fairies are said to dance at midnight on Midsummer Eve; and Torbery Hill near South Harting, another fairy dancing ground. South Cadbury Castle (Somerset), famed for its association with King Arthur, is a hillfort where the fairies were said to live, but they left when bells were put into the church (it is a worldwide tradition that evil spirits can be frightened away by the ringing of bells and other loud noises).

Two of the fairy occupants of a fort in Cumbria, on Castle Howe at Bassenthwaite, were seen after the discovery of a hut with a slate roof by some children who were digging into the hill with spades. After lunch they could not find the hut, though their spades were lying where they had left them. No one was seen, but a few days later two tiny men dressed in green were spotted by the children's father on top of the hill. He set his dog on to them, but it was stopped by a mysterious force, and nervously returned to its master. The men disappeared into the ground. Another version tells of a man who stumbled in the hillfort ruins as he climbed Castle Howe, and overturned a boulder. He glanced back—and saw a little man dressed in green sitting on the boulder. But when he turned to look again, the fairy was gone. The name 'The Fairy Glen' has been given to the flat top of Castle Howe, but it is said that this name did not originate as a result of the fairy sighting. Also said to be a fairy haunt was the camp Beacon Ring on Long Mountain (Salop), while Cow Castle on Exmoor (in Devon) was built by the fairies as a protection against the earth-spirits.

Fairies were traditionally fond of music and merry-making, so it is not surprising that stories have persisted about mounds where the curious will be able to hear fairy music. The Music Barrow on Bincombe Down (Dorset) is one such mound, and midday is the time to put your ear close to the ground there. The fairies of Durham were particularly enthusiastic musicians, according to this quotation from *Legends and Superstitions of the County of Durham* by William Brockie:

The fairies usually took up their abode during the day underground in the bosom of isolated round green hills, I have met with people who knew this to be a fact, because sometimes on a fine still summer evening, when they had lain down on these hills with their ear close to the ground, they were astonished to hear piping, fiddling, singing, and dancing going on far down in the interior. When questioned as to whether the sounds might not rather come from some neighbouring village or gipsy encampment, they would reply that that was quite impossible. 'No' they replied, 'it certainly was the fairies; everybody knew it was;

hundreds had heard them; there could be no doubt it was the fairies.' Indeed almost every circular mound in the North must once have been thus used, if all tales be true.

The curiosity of a piper wishing to learn the fairies' tunes was his downfall, for he went into the Picts' Knowe (afterwards called Piper's Grave) near Ednam (Borders: Roxburgh) and never came out again.

Burial mounds and hillforts were not the only ancient sites frequented by the fairies; they were also seen at certain stones, for example the Pentre Ifan cromlech (Dyfed: Pembroke), where they looked like 'little children in clothes like soldiers' clothes and with red caps'. Another Welsh cromlech associated with fairies is near the hamlet of St Nicholas (South Glamorgan) and was called Castle Correg by the local children. Again in Wales, a stone at Cynwyl Gaio had a bad reputation and was known locally as the Goblin Stone. A young man who slept under it in the seventeenth century was pinched, poked, and tweaked by a number of goblins, who vanished at first light.

Fairies were known to dance at night round the King Stone, part of the Rollright group of stones on the Oxfordshire/Warwickshire border, and an old man who claimed to have actually seen them described them as 'little folk like girls to look at'. This same man's widow remembered that the fairies were supposed to come out of a hole in the bank near the King Stone. She and her friends had often placed a stone over the hole in order to stop the fairies coming out, and had always found it disturbed the next morning. The fairies were also known to dance around the Witch's Stone, near the slate quarries near Aberfoyle (Central: Perth), and the name of this stone may indicate the identity of this particular class of fairies: they might have been witches engaged in their ritual dances.

Other traditions associating fairies with ancient stones may have resulted from the psychic effects produced by the earth currents. These are the tales of a stone being the gateway to fairyland, as, for example, described in this extract from *Folk Lore of East Yorkshire* by John Nicholson:

About half way down the hill forming the eastern slope of Nafferton Slack [now in Humberside], by the road-side, to prevent waggons leaving the roadway, stood a large stone, which was believed to have wonderful powers. At night, at certain seasons, it glowed like fire, sometimes it seemed but the portal of a well-lighted hall; and one old stone-breaker declared he had heard wonderful music issuing therefrom, the like of which he had never heard before; while on one occasion he had seen troops of gaily-dressed elfins repairing thither, some on foot and some in carriages, and they all went into this mysterious hall. The old man is dead, the stone is gone, and the fairies have departed.

A similar story comes from Wales, and tells of a shepherd boy, lost in the mountains, who was led to a certain menhir by a merry blue-eyed old man. The old man tapped three times on the stone and lifted it up, revealing steps lit by a blue-white light. Down they went, and came to a wooded, fertile country with a beautiful palace. The shepherd boy began a marvellous life among the 'fair-folk', and eventually married one of them. Later, he decided to return to the upper world and took his wife with him. They lived well, for they were rich, and had a son they called Taliesin, who became a famous bard. This story may have been a remnant of an ancient bardic tale. The wooded fertile country, where life is joyous and riches abound, to which an ancient sacred stone is the doorway, may symbolise the fructifying powers of the earth current which can be tapped at ancient stones.

Another possible link between fairies and the current that may flow through the earth has already been mentioned in Chapter One—the Irish fairy paths. The description of them in the following quotation from W. Y. Evans Wentz's *The Fairy-Faith in Celtic Countries* clearly shows the power of the current, and the necessity of placing a house on the best site in order to receive the beneficial effects and avoid the deleterious—an ability completely lost today. This quotation also contains warnings to all who contemplate interfering with ancient sites in any way. (Many other examples of such beliefs will be given in Chapter Eight.) The speaker is a Roman Catholic priest from the west of Ireland, one of many people who recounted their knowledge of fairy lore to Evans Wentz when he toured the British Isles for this purpose in the first years of this century.

'A heap of stones in a field should not be disturbed, though needed for building—especially if they are part of an ancient tumulus. The fairies are said to live inside the pile and to move the stones would be most unfortunate.

'If a house happens to be built on a fairy-preserve, or in a fairy-track, the occupants will have no luck. Everything will go wrong. Their animals will die, their children fall sick, and no end of trouble will come on them. When the house happens to have been built in a fairy-track, the doors on the front and back, or the windows if they are in the line of the track, cannot be kept closed at night, for the fairies must march through.

'Near Ballinrobe [Mayo] there is an old fort which is still the preserve of the fairies, and the land around it. The soil is very fine and yet no one would dare to till it. Some time ago in laying out a new road the engineers determined to run it through the fort, but the people rose almost in rebellion and the course had to be changed. The farmers wouldn't cut down a tree or bush growing on the hill or preserve for anything.'

We have not so far mentioned any of the many ways in which the fairies were said to interact with human beings, because ancient sites were rarely involved, but three exceptions are noted here. The first is the story of Wick Barrow, or Pixy Mound, near Stogursey (Somerset). This is now, thanks to progress, close to a nuclear power station, and a more unpleasant location we have yet to visit. The story tells of a ploughman who found a tiny wooden baker's peel with a broken handle lying on the mound. He thought it was a child's toy spade and so he mended it and left it where he had found it. Later he returned to see if the spade was still there, and found instead a cake which he ate, and thereafter the ploughman prospered. Another story of services rendered comes from Scotland, but this time it is the Little People who help humans. Near Ben Loyal (near Tongue, Highland: Sutherland) is a stone called the Stone of the Little Men, and anyone leaving a silver coin and a model or drawing of the metal object required will, in a week's time, find a perfect one made by the dwarfs in their smelting furnace at the heart of Ben Loyal. A fairy smith was in business at Wayland's Smithy, a chambered barrow near Uffington (Oxfordshire). In 1738 Francis Wise told the tale thus:

At this place lived formerly an invisible Smith; and if a traveller's horse had lost a shoe upon the road, he had no more to do than to bring the horse to this place, with a piece of money, and leaving both there for some time, he might come again and find the money gone, but the horse new shod.

The study of fairy lore is complex: each writer on the subject often favours a different explanation to cover the whole range of traditions. In fact a wide reading of the happenings lumped together under the heading 'fairies' rather indicates that all eight of the explanations given earlier are valid, and there is no one source for all fairy lore.

If we relate the diverse material outlined so far in this chapter to the theory of earth currents, the following emerges. Fairies would seem to be attracted to ancient sites of all kinds, but especially to earthen forts (where they often live) and to stone circles or standing stones (where they dance). The fairyland sometimes glimpsed by mere mortals may be a symbol of the current at the site; or it may be an actual hallucination experienced at the site, caused by a sudden excessive intake of current—a temporary insight into other realms, as sometimes occurs in altered states of consciousness. The stories of mortals joining fairies in their dances and losing awareness of earth-time, emerging apparently only minutes later to find years elapsed, may simply be indications of the power of the earth current, its ability to overwhelm the senses of the inexperienced, to cause temporal and spatial dislocation. Here is just one example (quoted from Evans Wentz's *The Fairy-Faith in Celtic Countries*) from the many to be found in books of folklore. The speaker is Donald Mc. Kinnon, who was a ninety-six-year-old piper, the oldest man on the island of Barra (Western Isles) when he spoke to Evans Wentz.

The impressive front façade of Wayland's Smithy chambered tomb.

'I heard of another man to whom a child was born; and as it was customary then as it is now-a-days on such occasions, the man went for some whiskey. On his return with a small cask of it on his back he saw a fairy-residence open and went into it. He began to converse with the fairies and it wasn't long before they wanted him to dance with them. He did so; and after passing what in his opinion

was a few hours there, a fairy-man said to him, *It is now time for you to be going, for you have been here a year.*

'His family had given up all hopes of ever seeing him again. The prevalent opinion was that he was either killed on the road or else had fallen in with some mortal accident. And so when he appeared in his own home again the terrification of his people was extreme, and it was only on his relating his experience with the fairies that his wife and the rest of the family came to understand. And he on his part was equally surprised when he saw his baby walking.'

Witches

Witches sometimes used to gather at certain stones for their assemblies or Sabbats, and the chosen stones often had a part to play in the proceedings. The memory of witches' Sabbats being held at stone circles sometimes remains in a tradition attached to the site, which says that the stones are women who were turned to stone for dancing on the Sabbath. Some examples of these traditions were given in Chapter Four.

It seems likely that the practices of medieval witches derived from pre-Christian rituals, but, as with all the old traditions recorded in this book, the necessary words and actions had degenerated over the centuries until their true meaning (and probably also their efficacy) had been lost, only a mimetic parody of the original being left. T. C. Lethbridge felt, as already mentioned in Chapter One, that the dances performed by witches at stone circles were intended to build up power which could be stored in the stones, but it is impossible to know how effective the rituals were. The witches were always very secretive about what they were doing, and even when tortured to extract confessions rarely gave much away; that is assuming that they really were practising witches (which many victims of the witch hunts were not) and that they understood the real significance of their practices. Margaret A. Murray, in *The Witch-Cult in Western Europe*, tells us that the witches' dances were intended to promote fertility, and that the form of the dance varied according to whether the fertility of crops, animals, or humans was involved.

The witches also resorted to ancient stones in order to work spells and charms, and in this respect their behaviour differs little from that of the ordinary folk who followed traditional rituals at certain sites in order to achieve their desires. In a witch trial at Auldearn (Highland: Nairn) in 1662 a witch confessed that she and her cronies were wont to raise the wind at the Kempock Stane (Strathclyde: Renfrew):

When we raise the wind we take a rag of cloth and wet it in water, and we take a beetle [mallet] and knock the rag on a stone and we say thrice over—

This graphic woodcut shows a witch creating a storm at sea.

I knock this rag upon this stane,
To raise the wind in the devil's name.
It shall not lie until I please again.

Frequently one finds witch lore bound up with fairy lore. In witches' confessions there is often mention of obtaining help and secret powers from the fairies at their earthen dwellings. In 1566 the examination of John Walsh of Netherbury (Dorset) revealed that he visited the fairies:

He being demaunded how he knoweth when anye man is bewytched: He sayth that he knew it partlye by the Feries, and saith that ther be .iii. kindes of Feries, white, greene, and black. Which when he is disposed to vse, hee speaketh with them vpon hyls, where as there is great heapes of earth, as namely in Dorsetshire. And betwene the houres of .xii. and one at noone, or at midnight he vseth them. Whereof (he sayth) the blacke Feries be the woorst.

A Yorkshireman, apprehended in 1653 on suspicion of witchcraft, told how he became involved with the fairies, through meeting 'a fair Woman in fine cloaths' when he was 'very sad and full of heavy thoughts'. She said she would help him to get a good living by helping to cure the sick, and

she led him to a little hill and she knocked three times, and the Hill opened, and they went in, and came to a fair hall, wherein was a Queen sitting in great state, and many people about her, and the Gentlewoman that brought him, presented him to the Queen, and she said he was welcom, and bid the Gentlewoman give him some of the white powder, and teach him how to use it, which she did, and gave him a little wood box full of the white powder, and bad him give 2 or 3 grains of it to any that were Sick, and it would heal them, and so she brought him forth of the Hill, and so they parted. And being asked by the Judge whether the place within the Hill, which he called a Hall, were light or dark, he said indifferent, as it is with us in the twilight; and being asked how he got more powder, he said when he wanted he went to that Hill, and knocked three times, and said every time I am coming, I am coming, whereupon it opened, and he going in was conducted by the aforesaid Woman to the Queen, and so had more powder given him.

Witches are just one link in the chain which connects the traditions extant today with the practices of prehistoric man. They helped to keep the old rituals alive long after their real meaning was lost, and some of the strange results they achieved were possibly due to the power of the earth currents, even though the witches attributed them to the Devil.

Ghosts

Ghosts are ubiquitous. Before we describe some of their appearances at ancient sites, and suggest what connection they might have with the flow of current, it might be helpful to give briefly some of the present beliefs regarding the nature of ghosts. The most widespread popular belief is that they are an evil manifestation of the dead, and this belief carries with it the supposition that ghosts are conscious in some way. The evidence gathered by psychic researchers strongly suggests that most ghosts can in fact be likened to images such as we see in television pictures or movie films. Such recorded images have no consciousness and have therefore neither good nor evil intent, and the films in which they are seen are simply playbacks of incidents which occurred at some time in the past. As it is not self-conscious, a ghost cannot respond to any attempt at communication (although there are some exceptional cases on record in which the ghostly image spoke; in such cases the sound would have been as subjective as the image). Therefore it is most likely that a ghost is a hallucination, the formation of which is triggered off in the percipient's brain by an external stimulus, possibly some type of 'impression' left on the 'ether' of the location by the person whose ghost is seen. Usually a strong emotion experienced by the individual who later appears as a ghost causes the 'impression' to be formed. In the majority of cases ghosts look like living people, solid

Overleaf:
The Avebury henge monument 'does as much exceed in greatness the so renowned Stonehenge, as a Cathedral does a parish Church', wrote John Aubrey about 1663. It is still impressive 300 years later, and careful restoration of certain sections, including the south-west quadrant shown here, enables us to gain some idea of how the site must have looked in Neolithic and Bronze Age times.

and three-dimensional, and in fact look so real that only unnatural behaviour, such as walking through a wall, tells the percipient that there is something odd going on! However, not all 'ghosts' recorded at ancient sites fit this description, and it would seem that often what is seen or experienced is not a ghost as such, but an elemental force manifesting itself in a form which is often frightening to see.

The ghost who has been seen at a round barrow near Squirrel's Corner, not far from Cranborne (Dorset), was a solid-looking apparition. He has been seen more than once, bare legged and wearing a long grey cloak, and riding fast without bridle or stirrups. An archaeologist, driving home from a dig one night, watched him gallop alongside his car before vanishing by the round barrow. Another time, a shepherd saw him come from a clump of trees near a prehistoric camp and, unsuspecting, asked him for a light for his pipe, whereupon the horseman vanished!

On at least two occasions, people have witnessed activity among the stones of Avebury (Wiltshire) when there was really nothing to be seen. During the First World War, Edith Olivier, author of books on Wiltshire, was driving through Avebury at twilight and heard the music and saw the lights of a fair among the stones. When she later remarked on this, she was told that it was at least fifty years since a fair had been held there. On another occasion someone saw many small figures moving among the stones on a bright moonlit night, and described the feeling as 'most uncanny'. Also in Wiltshire, phantom cortèges have been seen on Wansdyke, the defensive frontier, possibly Anglo-Saxon, which runs across the southern part of the county for seven and a half miles. A hundred years ago a cortège was seen on the dyke near Huish, and on another occasion a party of men walking behind a wagon, which bore a coffin and was drawn by black horses, was seen one dark night by two shepherds and a boy at the point where the dyke runs to the north of Tan Hill in All Cannings parish. On top of the coffin was a crown, or it may have been a circle of gold. The apparition vanished when it drew level with the shepherds.

All these reports are typical ghost stories that can be explained by the theory that what is seen by the percipients is a 're-run' of something which actually happened in the past. The interpretation of the next story is less certain, for it may be simply a fiction, a warning that anyone who interferes with ancient stones may be condemned to haunt the place of his folly. Or it may be an account of something which really happened. As we have remarked before in connection with folklore traditions, it is never easy to decide what actually happened and what did not, but there is probably some basis of truth in even the fictional stories. The ghost in this case was that of old Taylor, who could not rest because he had moved a landmark near the White Cross a mile out of Hereford city. One night a man fulfilled a promise to meet old Taylor's ghost at midnight at a place

The gold corselet found in the Hill of the Goblins near Mold.

called the Morning Pits, and the ghost led him to two huge stones nearby, ordering him to lift them. He did so, with surprising ease, and after he had carried them to the place pointed out by the ghost, he was sworn to silence and told to lie face down and not move until he heard music. He did as he was told, but the experience seems to have been too much for him, for shortly afterwards he died of fright.

The next two cases show how information retained in the collective folk memory may manifest itself in the form of a ghost story. Silbury Hill (Wiltshire), a truly enigmatic mound whose purpose is still not known, for no ancient burials have yet been discovered there despite investigations made for that specific reason, is said to be haunted on moonlit nights by King Sil on horseback. The local story is that King Sil is buried there, clad in golden armour and mounted on his horse. This may not be pure fantasy, if the case of the Hill of the Goblins (Bryn yr Ellyllon) near Mold (Clwyd: Flint) is any guide as to how much credence to place in old folk traditions. This cairn was long said to be haunted by a man in golden armour, and when the mound was cleared away in 1833, as already described in Chapter One, a gold corselet was found, together with a man's skeleton.

Sometimes ghostly manifestations at ancient sites take the form of vague, insubstantial disturbances, with nothing actually seen but noises heard and atmospheres felt. A lady was walking one summer's day on Walker's Hill, Alton Priors, Wiltshire. Her precise route was from the barrow (Adam's Grave) above the white horse to the layby at the top of the hill. Close to the barrow she felt suddenly uneasy, but could see no reason for this feeling: no one else was around, a flock of sheep was undisturbed. Then she heard horses' hooves thudding, enough for a whole army, but still nothing unusual could be seen. She quickened her step, and after she had passed Adam's Grave she could no longer hear the horses.

Interference with long-standing sites often brings about disturbances (as we will detail in Chapter Eight), and sometimes these are of an apparently psychic nature. In the following instance, a church was altered, and the resulting disturbance was definitely ghostly. The church was at Maughold on the Isle of Man, and it was decided to make two steps up to the communion rails instead of one steep one. During their excavations the labourers found bones buried beneath the step. These were dug up and left exposed at lunch-time, and one labourer who stayed in the church heard distinct sounds of whispering or murmuring all over the church. The bones were reinterred promptly, and the whispering ceased.

The next few cases describe what may be elementals: they are certainly not typical 'ghosts'! The first, 'the most terrifying thing he had ever seen', according to the witness, most certainly was not a ghost. E. Dauncey Tongue believed that what he saw near Hangley Cleeve Barrows in Somerset in 1908 was a 'Barrow Guardian', and twenty years later he still spoke of the sight as 'terrifying', even though by that time he was a District Commissioner and big-game hunter in East Africa. What he actually saw he described as 'a crouching form like a rock with matted hair all over it, and pale, flat eyes'.

Equally terrifying is the story of an indescribable 'something' encountered by a doctor in Written Stone Lane, near Longridge (Lancashire). Late one night he was riding past the Written Stone (which is described more fully, and illustrated, in Chapter Eight) when his horse became hysterical, and took off at a gallop, only stopping two miles farther on. The doctor must have been feeling especially bold, for, despite this adventure, he decided to return to the Written Stone and face whatever had frightened the horse. He rode up to the stone and issued a challenge, whereupon, in the words of Kathleen Eyre, describing the encounter in her *Lancashire Legends*, 'a shapeless mass materialised, seized him, plucked him from the saddle and almost squeezed the breath from his body'. As soon as he was able, the doctor left the spot at a gallop. Traditionally the stone marks the site of a cruel murder, and was put there 'to appease the restless spirit of the deceased'.

Spectral dogs are frequently recorded as being seen at ancient sites, but they could never be mistaken for normal dogs, and therefore are unlikely to be simply ghosts of dogs no longer living. We do not know what they are, or why a *dog* should so often appear in horrific guise. Many areas of the British Isles have their spectral black dogs, and each area has its own local name for them—Black Shuck in East Anglia, the Barguest in Yorkshire, the Trash-hound in Lancashire, the Gwyllgi in Wales, Tchi-co on Guernsey, Le Tchan de Bouole on Jersey, Mauthe Doog in the Isle of Man, and the Pooka in Ireland. The many reports of spectral black dogs are by no means always pure fantasy, for there are among them some firsthand accounts of calf-size black dogs with glowing eyes that have been seen in recent years.

The ghostly dog seen on the island of Anglesey (Gwynedd) by a clergyman took the form of a large greyhound. It jumped against him and threw him from his horse as he passed by an 'artificial circle in the ground' (presumably of stones, to judge by what occurs later) between Amlwch village and St Elian church. The same thing happened on a second night; on the third the priest saw that the 'spirit' was chained. On being questioned, the 'spirit' revealed that it could not rest because it had, when in the flesh (presumably in human not animal form!) hidden a silver groat belonging to the church under a stone. Following the 'spirit's' directions, the priest found the groat and paid it to the church, whereupon the 'spirit' was released.

The next story also comes from Wales, and we quote it direct from *Folk-Lore of West and Mid-Wales* by Jonathan Ceredig Davies:

As Mr. David Walter, of Pembrokeshire, a religious man, and far from fear and superstition, was travelling by himself through a field called the Cot Moor, where there are two stones set up called the Devil's Nags, which are said to be haunted, he was suddenly seized and thrown over a hedge. He went there another day, taking with him for protection a strong fighting mastiff dog. When he had come near the Devil's Nags there appeared in his path the apparition of a dog more terrible than any he had ever seen. In vain he tried to set his mastiff on: the huge beast crouched, frightened by his master's feet and refused to attack the spectre. Whereupon his master boldly stooped to pick up a stone thinking that would frighten the evil dog; but suddenly a circle of fire surrounded it, which lighting up the gloom, showed the white snip down to the dog's nose, and his grinning teeth, and white tail. He then knew it was one of the infernal dogs of hell.

Black dogs seen near barrows in Somerset, such as Wambarrow near Dulverton, are regarded as treasure guardians. Whiteborough, a large tumulus on St Stephen's Down near Launceston (Cornwall), was believed

The burial chamber inside West Kennet long barrow.

to conceal giants' treasure, and on one occasion a ghostly black dog appeared to men who had just been taking part in a wrestling match there. In Wiltshire, Doghill Barrow on Knighton Down, near Stonehenge, has its ghostly dog (which came first, the ghost or the barrow's name?), while in the same county two sizable burial chambers are frequented by huge white dogs. West Kennet long barrow is said to be entered at sunrise on the longest day by a 'priest' followed by a huge white hound with red 'ears' (could this be a mistake for 'eyes', resulting from the frequent retelling of the story?). Devil's Den, a dolmen near Fyfield, is the site of an unsuccessful removal attempt by the Devil, who at midnight tries to move the heavy capstone. During his struggle a huge white dog 'with eyes of burning coals' stands by.

It is possible that the ability to perceive these ghosts and elemental creatures, sometimes experienced by mere mortals, could stem from the energy of the earth currents that flow through the ancient sites. Neurophysiologists have found by experiment that a brain, if artificially stimulated by electrical impulses, will react by producing its own hallucinatory responses, and whether of a visible, audible, or olfactory nature will depend on the area of the brain which has been stimulated. We believe that similar stimulation may on occasion take place by means of the earth currents. This could happen when all the conditions involving the strength and direction of the currents and the state of responsiveness of the percipient's brain are in accord. If this suggestion seems too outrageous to be acceptable, the reader is at liberty to devise his own. What cannot be done is to reject as meaningless the great body of tradition which states that throughout all ages many people have experienced the inexplicable.

UFOs

From time to time it has been suggested that UFOs 'use' ley lines and the earth currents—that they can 'lock on to' the leys as a navigation aid; that they somehow use the earth currents to power their craft; that they materialise or dematerialise with the aid of the earth currents. But no strong evidence has been put forward in support of any of these theories, and in fact it is doubtful if such evidence could ever be produced, simply because of the nature of the circumstances. Most moving UFOs are some distance above the ground, also they are generally seen at night, often only briefly, and the witness is rarely in a calm frame of mind. Therefore it is not possible to determine exactly the route taken by a UFO. Even if it were proposed that one particular UFO had followed a ley, might it not be possible that coincidence only was involved? Without prior warning of the UFO's appearance, and then careful tracking of its route by scientific methods, the suggestion that UFOs follow leys cannot be proved.

Similarly there is as yet no strong evidence that UFOs are particularly interested in ancient sites, and again such interest would be hard to prove. An occasional witnessed fly-over might be pure coincidence; closer visits and possible landings are likely to be undertaken circumspectly and at night, as with most low-level UFO activity. (Non-readers of specialised UFO reports are usually amazed to learn how many actual landings, and sightings of UFO occupants, have been recorded in the past thirty years all over the world, many of them being investigated, and most pronounced genuine, by competent investigators.) As the majority of ancient sites are not close to areas of human occupation, much could happen there which would not be observed. Until positive evidence comes to light, we can do no more than record the possibility that UFOs may take an interest in ancient sites. If they do it would not be surprising in view of the suggestions now being made by individuals of integrity who have spent much time investigating this phenomenon, that UFOs are not simply solid craft from other planets, but psychic manifestations able to be material or non-material as the occasion demands, coming from who knows what other dimensions.

We include here as of possible relevance two UFO cases. The better of the two is, unfortunately, not from the British Isles, but at least it shows that it is not outside the bounds of possibility that UFOs visit ancient sites. First the English case, which comes from Dorset. There is an Iron Age hillfort on Eggardon Hill near Bridport, and it was above the hill that Michael Byatt saw a yellow-blue light in the sky in the form of an eclipse (*sic*). His attention was drawn to the light when, driving over the hill one night in September 1974, his car's engine began to lose power and his lights dimmed. It became intensely cold, and afterwards Mr Byatt and his passenger described 'an eerie presence'. The light 'moved slowly backwards and forwards' and had 'a sort of glow about it', and Mr Byatt, a registered gliding instructor and senior NCO in the Air Training Corps, was unable to equate it with any known flying object. On another occasion, a couple of years earlier, three cars climbing the hill at night had all stopped suddenly at the same time, with loss of power and lights, but everything returned to normal in a short while. Readers of UFO reports will know that such electrical failures in vehicles are common when UFOs are close by, though they do not always happen.

The other UFO sighting took place on the Italian island of Sardinia, and the details are taken from 'An early Italian cross-country case' by Mary Boyd (*Flying Saucer Review**, vol. 20, no. 3). There are a number of

* FSR Publications Ltd, West Malling, Maidstone, Kent.

nuraghi (prehistoric fortified dwellings resembling dolmens) in the district of Caglieri, and this particular one was at Trudumeddu. One afternoon in May 1931 the two eye-witnesses were horse-riding in the area and as they were admiring the view a 'strange object emerged from the partially blocked entrance of the *nuraghe* standing in the middle of the field'. It was spherical in shape and looked like 'a brand-new football'. (UFOs come in all shapes and sizes; the variety in the objects seen is just one aspect of a complex study.) One of the men followed it on foot as it travelled away about one metre above the ground at a speed estimated at between sixteen and twenty kilometres per hour. After crossing the field in a straight line it entered a stand of bushes and undergrowth, and the witness noticed that 'the undergrowth parted in front of the "football", and the bushes bent over, but once it had passed on they closed and straightened up again. In other words, they opened up a passageway *before* coming in contact with it, as though displaced by a mysterious and invisible force that preceded the flying object.' The man chasing after it was unable to overtake it, and his friend kept shouting to him to come back, so he gave up the chase when the 'football' vanished amid thick undergrowth. The two men did not enter the *nuraghe* because of the second man's terror, and so we have no clues as to what the strange object was doing there.

8 The fate of the desecrators

To disturb an ancient site or remove an old stone was to invite disaster. There are many traditions which give warnings to would-be desecrators and others telling what befell those who disregarded the warnings. At the beginning of this century a farmer in the townland of Rathmore (Kerry) was mowing his grassland and feeling annoyed because he could not get his mowing machine in between the banks of a fort on his land. He decided to get his sons to level the banks, and next day the work began. When the men stopped to light a pipe, their horse and cart were close by. They turned their backs to the wind for no more than thirty seconds, but what they saw when they had lit their pipes amazed them. For the horse was out of its shafts and grazing quietly. A horse and cart are noisy in movement, but the separation of horse from cart had happened in absolute silence in less than half a minute! As D. A. Mac Manus comments on this strange story in *The Middle Kingdom*,

Here was unexpected intervention by the unseen world which could not be ignored, and neither of the lads was in the slightest doubt as to its meaning. It was an unmistakable but fortunately a very gentle and kindly warning not to tamper further with or desecrate in any way this fort now clearly appropriated to the fairies' use. It is not surprising, then, that in a few moments the boys were on their way home with the horse and cart. When they told their adventures to their father, their quite obvious sincerity and distress soon convinced him of the truth of their story. That bank still remains inviolate to this very day and can be seen at any time by the sufficiently curious. [written 1959]

This Irish farmer had a mild warning not to interfere. Usually more unpleasant events occurred: sickness or death of animals or people, strange voices, poltergeists, and weather disturbances in particular, and we have many examples of these to relate. Reasons for disturbing ancient sites vary: farmers may wish to remove stones or level earthworks in order to cultivate every foot of land, and to remove obstructions to the easy use of their farm machinery; treasure-seekers may dig into mounds in search of riches; country people may take stones to use in the building of houses, walls and pigsties, or as gateposts. Whatever the reason, it is invariably selfish, and inevitably, those whose motives are selfish are not, in the long run, the happiest of people. In the old stories the transgressors usually got their just deserts without delay, as in the following tale of a man who went with other treasure-seekers to dig for gold under a menhir near Fowey (Cornwall).

Wherefore, in a faire moone-shine night, thither with certaine good fellowes hee hyeth to dig it up. A working they fall, their labour shortneth, their hope increaseth, a pot of gold is the least of their expectation. But see the chance. In midst of their toyling the skie gathereth clouds, the moonelight is overcast with darknesse,

One of the Bronze Age round barrows known as Robin Hood's Butts.

downe fals a mightie showre, up riseth a blustering tempest, the thunder cracketh, the lightning flasheth. In conclusion, our money-seekers washed instead of loden, or loden with water instead of yellow earth, and more afraid than hurt, are forced to abandon their enterprise and seeke shelter of the next house they could get into.

More subtle but equally effective was the thwarting of treasure-seekers at Robin Hood's Butts, a number of round barrows in the Blackdown Hills of Somerset. A rich man who wanted the treasure reputedly hidden in one of the barrows set workmen to dig for it, but after a day's hard work, digging trenches and carting away earth, the barrow seemed no smaller. They left stakes to mark their finishing point, but next morning they returned to find no traces of the previous day's work—trenches and piles of earth had disappeared, and gorse was growing in their place. The workmen ran off, so the rich man decided to dig for himself. He began to dig a trench, but when he stopped to look at his work, no hole could be seen. He gave up!

Sometimes, however, if the need was great and genuine, the treasure would be found, as is supposed to have happened on Pentyrch, a hill above Llangybi (Gwynedd: Caernarvon). A large stone, immovable despite the concerted efforts of men and horses on many occasions, was moved at the touch of a little girl's hand. She found a hoard of coins beneath the stone, and at the time her family was desperately poor. It had long been rumoured that treasure was hidden there, but undeserving seekers had had no luck finding it.

It is clear that the people regarded these sites as sacrosanct, and as embodying a power of revenge against anyone foolhardy enough to inter-fere with them. If we apply the theory of earth currents to this belief, an explanation for the multiplicity of disasters recorded in the traditions would appear to be that the flow of earth current still existing in many of the ancient sites is disturbed if the site is disturbed, and its involuntary release by inexperienced persons produces an uncontrolled outburst of energy which can cause harm to nearby people and animals, and disrupt the weather. The effects are not always harmful, though, according to a tradition from County Mayo in Ireland. This tells of a stone-built giant's grave on a wild mountainside (location not given). If anyone were to dig into the grave, the mountainside would immediately be changed into a fertile plain, and a key buried in the tomb would open the gate of a beauti-ful city at the bottom of a nearby lake. Also the discoverer would have at his disposal 'a great golden treasure'. This allegory tells us what can happen if the pent-up current is handled correctly: that this current is the key to the well-being of the people, the fertility of the land, and spiritual riches.

Stones resistant to being moved

The lore of holy wells would make a book in itself, and so although many of these sacred pools and springs have probably been used and revered for centuries, and can therefore in that sense be classed as ancient sites, we are only referring to them when a holy well tradition is particularly relevant, as is the following. This version of the story is by T. Quiller-Couch (*Notes and Queries*, vol. x) and relates to St Nunn's, St Nun's, or St Ninnie's Well, Pelynt (Cornwall).

The stone trough at St Nun's Well can be seen through the doorway.

An old farmer once set his eyes upon the granite basin and coveted it; for it was not wrong in his eyes to convert the holy font to the base uses of the pig's stye; and accordingly he drove his oxen and wain to the gateway above for the purpose of removing it. Taking his beasts to the entrance of the well, he essayed to drag the trough from its ancient bed. For a long time it resisted the efforts of the oxen, but at length they succeeded in starting it, and dragged it slowly up the hill-side to where the wain was standing. Here, however, it burst away from the chains which held it, and, rolling back again to the well, made a sharp turn and regained

The stones aptly named the Whispering Knights were once the upright walls of a burial chamber.

its old position, where it has remained ever since. Nor will any one again attempt removal, seeing that the farmer, who was previously well-to-do in the world, never prospered from that day forward. Some people say, indeed, that retribution overtook him on the spot, the oxen falling dead, and the owner being struck lame and speechless.

The stones of Zennor Quoit, one of several impressive megalithic constructions variously known as quoits, dolmens, or cromlechs, are in the West Penwith area of Cornwall, and are said to be immovable, but the tradition contradicts itself by continuing, 'if anyone does move them they return to their former position by the following morning'!

Attempts were often made to move stones in order to get at the gold said to be hidden underneath. But only at certain times would such attempts be successful. The Cock-Crow Stone at Wellington (Somerset) turned round every time the cock crew, and if you happened to be on the spot at the right time, and the right cock was crowing, you might be lucky enough to push the stone aside and get at the gold. If it was the wrong cock or the wrong time, not even a team of horses could move the stone. Another stone which could move if the conditions were right, but which was averse to being forced to move, was the Wimblestone at Shipham in Somerset's Mendip Hills. A farmer with two horses wasted a whole day trying to move the stone, but that night it roamed around the Mendips, and visited the Waterstone at Wrington (presumably to relate to it the antics of the foolish farmer!). At Churchstanton in Somerset, a farmer gave up trying to move a stone, although he had been using his strongest horses in his treasure-seeking attempt. A stone at Culm Davy (Devon) is said to have money buried beneath it, but no one has yet been successful in moving the stone to find out if the story is true. The greed which motivates such efforts can sometimes rebound on to the seeker, as happened at the Caractacus Stone on Winsford Hill, Exmoor (Somerset). A wagoner who tried to move the stone to get at its treasure was crushed to death when the stone overturned, and now, on foggy nights, the ghosts of the wagoner and his team of horses haunt the spot.

The remains of a burial chamber in the group of sites at Rollright (Oxfordshire) is called the Whispering Knights, and its large capstone was once earmarked for use as a bridge across a stream. Several horses were required to drag the stone *downhill* to the stream, where it proved unsatisfactory as a bridge because it moved every night. So it was decided to return it whence it came, the *uphill* journey being accomplished easily using only one horse. The Devil's Stone near Chertsey (Surrey) is said to conceal a rich treasure, but no one can move the stone (which may mean that no one has the ability to utilise the power locked up inside the stone). A farmer tried to move the Winceby Boulder at Winceby (Lincolnshire), to obtain its treasure, but he got more than he bargained for. He had his horses yoked to the boulder with chains, and according to an account quoted in *Lincolnshire Folklore,*

'The stone moved in its bed, and looked like coming out altogether, when one of the men helping said, "Let God or the Devil come now for we have it!" Something appeared to be standing on the stone, all of a sudden, and it seems to have been The Old Lad himself, for he left his claw mark on the stone in evidence! Any way the stone fell back into its place, faster [firmer] than ever.'

On another occasion a black mouse ran from under the boulder and terrified the horses, so that they could not be made to pull at the stone. As it interfered with the ploughing, a hole was dug beside it and the stone tipped over and buried. The author of *Lincolnshire Folklore*, Ethel H. Rudkin, interviewed a man who had dug down to the stone in about 1916 when someone wished to see it. He said he had to dig down about three feet, and he gave a full description of what he found, so it seems that at least part of the tradition was correct. When Miss Rudkin asked the man if he knew the story about the attempt to move the boulder, he replied: 'Aye, six 'osses it took—it was true enough—but they didn't shift it!'

A very similar story was told about the Drake Stone at Anwick (Lincolnshire). A man who used oxen to move the stone to get at its treasure was unsuccessful: the chains snapped, the oxen collapsed, and the 'guardian-spirit of the treasure' in the form of a drake flew from under the stone, which fell back into its place. This happened in 1832, according to one account. The stone was eventually buried in a hole dug beside it, because it interfered with the ploughing; and in 1913 it was relocated, hauled up (in two pieces, because it had broken), and repositioned near the church-yard gate. Two drakes regularly seen sheltering beneath the stone gave it its name.

Another stone in Lincolnshire which got in the way of the plough was the Sack Stone at Fonaby near Caistor. The farmer determined to move it, but the horses were not strong enough and oxen had to be used. They dragged it slowly downhill into the farmyard, where it was used as a stand to enable the cattle to drink from a high water-trough. But the horses died, the cattle became ill, and the farmer's son too, so the stone, which was blamed for all this bad luck, was taken back up the hill—pulled easily by one old lame mare. Straightaway the bad luck ceased. But this was not the only instance of ill-effects resulting from the removal of the Sack Stone, and more can be found under the heading 'Death and disaster' later in this chapter.

The Written Stone, in Written Stone Lane between Longridge and Dilworth in Lancashire, carries a carved message which dates it to the seventeenth century:

> Ravffe Radcliffe Laid This
> Stone to Lye For Ever AD 1655

But the tales associated with it are the same as those told of many an old standing stone. This may be because the Written Stone was originally a standing stone, or because it was, intentionally or accidentally, placed on the site of a standing stone and therefore took over the older stone's energy current. The local tradition suggests that Radcliffe had the stone carved in order to quieten the restless spirit that plagued the nearby Radcliffe farmhouse after a murder had been committed on the spot where the stone now stands. Travellers spoke of 'bumpings and screechings,

The Written Stone, now looking deceptively peaceful.

scratchings and pinchings, of cloaks tweaked and hats plucked off' in the lane, and a ghostly encounter at the stone is described in Chapter Seven. It seems that a poltergeist was associated with the stone, for when a farmer (after the time of the Radcliffes) decided to use the slab in his dairy, chaos ensued. More details are given under the heading 'Poltergeists, noises, and voices' later in this chapter. Relevant to this particular section is the fact that it took six horses and many men to actually move the stone to the farmhouse—but it needed only one horse to take the stone back, uphill, to its home in the lane.

St Cleer holy well. Although the baptistery is mid-fifteenth century, the cross and some masonry in the building are older.

Stones which return

As we have just related, many stones were returned to their sites with far less effort than was required to remove them originally. There are also traditions of stones that are able to return to their original position of their own accord. A stone at Ebbsfleet (Pegwell Bay) in east Kent was revered because, it was said, St Augustine stepped on it when he landed in England. Wherever it was moved to, it was believed to be able to return to its original site. One of Cornwall's best-known holy wells, at St. Cleer, incorporates a small baptistery, and attempts have been made to remove some of its stones, but they have always returned at night, by some 'mysterious power'. Farmers who removed stones for wall-building from Simon's Barrow in the Blackdown Hills near Wellington (Somerset) always found that they were returned (by the Devil, it was said), and ill-luck was all that remained with the farmer, as a penalty for having disturbed the stones.

A heap of stones on the mountain Cefn Carn Cavall (or Cabal), near Builth (Powys: Brecknock), contains one magic stone which bears the footprint of King Arthur's dog Cabal, and no one who takes this stone away can keep it for longer than a day and night, because it returns to the heap. On the island of Anglesey (Gwynedd), Maen Morddwyd, or the Thigh Stone, always returned the following night, however far away it was taken. During the reign of Henry I, Hugh, Earl of Chester, wished to test the tradition and had the stone chained to a larger stone and thrown into the sea. The next morning it was found in its usual place, so the Earl issued an edict ordering that no one should move it. One man, however, tied it to his thigh, whereupon his thigh turned putrid and the stone returned to its normal place. Its power waned, though, for it was eventually stolen and never returned.

A stone cross by St Munricha's Well, Aboyne (Grampian: Aberdeen), always came back if removed, as did Smig Mhic Mharcuis (The Chin of Mac Marquis), a piece of basalt which until early this century lay on a flat stone tomb in Kilbrandon graveyard on Seil in the Slate Isles (Strathclyde: Argyll). The 'chin' was said to turn so that it always pointed to the most recent grave.

The Butter Rolls, small pebbles on a stone near the old church of Fernagh in County Kerry (described more fully in Chapter Two), always returned if removed. A young lad who tried to steal one found that his horse refused to cross the bridge out of the parish, so he wisely returned the stone. A polished blue stone on one of the gravestones in the ruins of Temple Molaga, townland of Athacross (Cork), always returns if moved; and so do the round stones piled on a slab called the Bishop's Grave in a field near the graveyard of Foyoges (Sligo). On one occasion a man hurled two of the stones on to the rocky bed of a stream, breaking them in pieces, but next morning the pieces were back on the slab. The Summaghan Stones at Ballysummaghan, also in County Sligo, were seven cursing stones which reappeared in their usual place the morning after being thrown into the lake. A magical stone at Altagore (Antrim), called Shanven, 'the old woman', stood in a cottage garden and food was left on it for the 'grogan' or fairy. It was once made into a gatepost by a mason who did not know it was a magical stone, but next morning it was found standing in its usual place. The simplest explanation for traditions of this kind is that some of the local people venerated these stones so much that they were prepared to go to great lengths to preserve them and restore them to their rightful positions.

Death and disaster

Farmers in earlier centuries were often loth to disturb ancient stones and mounds for fear of what might happen. As late as 1859 a Manx farmer sacrificed a heifer, because he had allowed excavation to take place in a tumulus on his land, and naturally he wished to try and avert any consequences. These consequences could take a number of different forms, and reports of storms and poltergeist phenomena will be related later. Here we describe cases involving the illness, and sometimes death, of men and animals. Occasionally the stone being moved is the actual cause of death, as at Orchardleigh in Somerset where workmen were digging up a stone. They had reached a depth of ten feet and still the stone stood firm. Suddenly it fell and crushed one of the men; but then it immediately returned to its original position. This was in east Somerset. Across the other side of the county a farmer and his three sons who took a capstone from a burial chamber were soon all victims of their folly: one died of a fever, another was drowned, and the farmer and his remaining son were crushed by the stone as they were trying to incorporate it in their barn.

More often, the mystery illness or sudden death happens afterwards, forty-eight hours later in the case of the moving of the Arpafeelie basin stone by two local people. This stone lies embedded in the ground in a beechwood near Arpafeelie, Black Isle (Highland: Ross and Cromarty), and there is a local tradition that it must not be moved, for ill-luck will be the lot of anyone disturbing it. In 1937 permission was given by the owner of the estate where the stone lies to remove it to the museum at Inverness, and two people who went to examine it turned it over and forgot to put it back. Two days later, the family living at a nearby farm received news that a child relative had been killed in an accident, and a sheep farmer living at the same farm collapsed. As a result, the owner of the estate decided that the stone should not be removed to the museum after all. In this case the misfortune did not strike those who disturbed the stone, but some apparently unconnected people. In fact the farm whose inhabitants were afflicted is featured in another story concerning the moving of this stone a number of years before, and this we will retell later in this chapter. Perhaps there was a link between stone and farm which caused any misfortune to be focused on the occupants of the latter.

Mound-excavation seems to have been particularly hazardous, and in one case from Orkney a 'mound-dweller' angrily threatened a farmer who was opening a mound in one of his fields. As reported in the *Old Lore Miscellany* for July 1911 by the farmer's son-in-law, the mound-dweller was 'an old, grey-whiskered man dressed in an old, grey, tattered suit of clothes, patched in every conceivable manner, with an old bonnet in his hand, and old shoes of horse or cowhide tied on with strips of skin on his feet'. His words to the farmer were, as closely as could be remembered:

... thou are working thy own ruin, believe me, fellow, for if thou does any more work, thou will regret it when it is too late. Take me word, fellow, drop working in my house, for if thou doesn't, mark my word, fellow, if thou takes another shule-ful [shovelful], mark me word, thou will have six of the cattle deean in thy corn-yard at one time. And if thou goes on doing any more work, fellow—mark me word, fellow, thou will have then six funerals from the house, fellow; does thou mark me words; good-day, fellow ...

The speaker was never seen again, but, just as he had threatened, six cattle died, and also six members of the household.

The Torr mo Ghuidhe, or Hillock of my Wish, a mound in the Highlands between Bonar Bridge and Altas on the borders of the old counties of Sutherland and Ross and Cromarty, was protected by the belief that any-one who dug into it would be dead within a year, and a similar protection must have been in force on the island of Islay (Strathclyde: Argyll), where three people went mad after trying to open an ancient burial mound marked by a standing stone. The story does not say whether they were treasure-hunting, but this pursuit can also bring undesirable effects, as has already been shown. These are often in the form of bad weather, but sometimes worse afflictions befell the gold-greedy diggers. A man treasure-hunting in Broken Barrow on that part of Exmoor which is in Devon found a pot of ashes and bones, which he took away with him. Soon he became blind and deaf, and he died in less than three months. Castle Neroche in Somerset was traditionally said to be hollow and full of treasure and so was naturally the site of several digs. No one found the treasure, but most seem to have found something far less desirable, and this account by the Reverend F. Warre in 1854 (in *Proceedings*, Somerset, 5, i, 30 ff.) tells of one such unfortunate gang.

About a hundred years ago, a number of labouring men, urged on by the love of filthy lucre and not having the fear of archaeological societies before their eyes ... with sacrilegious spade and pick axe violated the sanctity of this mysterious hill. But before they had found a single coin they were seized with a panic fear, re-nounced their presumptuous enterprise and, wonderful and awful to relate, within one month of the commencement of their enterprise, some by accident, some by sudden death, and some by violent fevers, all paid with their lives the penalty of their covetous and most presumptuous attempt. Oh! that this most veracious legend were universally published as a warning to all wanton mutila-tors of ancient earthworks.

In the 1840s in Lincolnshire, Pelham's Pillar was being erected not far from the Sack Stone at Fonaby. One of the masons working on the pillar

Castle Neroche.

took a piece from the Sack Stone in order to model a small version of the
pillar: soon afterwards he fell from the pillar and broke his neck. Despite
a tradition that to try to move the stone would bring disaster, a farmer
broke off the top part of the Hoston Stone at Humberstone near Leicester
and filled in an associated ditch to facilitate ploughing. Originally owning
120 acres, he was eventually reduced to poverty, and died in the work-
house around 1800. With his 'punishment' spread over many years, a
definite connection between this farmer's fate and his interference with
the Hoston Stone can only be conjectured. But on the Isle of Man the
effects felt by two men who were employed to remove stones from a circle
at The Braid in Braddan parish were much more immediate. Straight
away on starting work they had terrible pains, one in his leg and the other
in his arm. Both went home, but it was too late: the afflicted limbs were
useless for the rest of their lives. They were lucky, however. A farmer who
began levelling a *keeill* (a small, early Christian chapel) on Camlork Farm,

also on the Isle of Man, had a pain in his arm which caused him to stop work, and when he went back to the job he was helped by his wife and daughter. They both died soon after, and the farmer went mad.

Animals are particularly sensitive to the emanations from ancient sites, and seem to be aware of the currents flowing through or present in stones. When a farmer took a stone from a stone circle on Loch nan Carrigean, Granish Moor, near Aviemore (Highland: Inverness), and made it into a lintel for his cowshed door, the cattle would not go under it, and his bull led him a merry dance through the fields. But when a new stone (presumably not from the stone circle) was substituted, there was no further trouble. On the Isle of Man, where a farmer similarly used a large stone (from a burial mound) as a lintel, his cow became ill, a calf died, and a hen was found dead on the nest. All was well again when he replaced the stone in the mound. Again on the Isle of Man, a farmer who built a small windmill of stones from a nearby *keeill* found that it had to be dismantled because when working it shook all the buildings violently. Worse, four cattle and three horses belonging to the farmer died of disease in a short space of time. A *keeill* was to blame for another mishap on the island, when in the parish of Jurby a farmer who drove his sheep into a *keeill* during a heavy thunderstorm found that in the following spring he lost all the lambs from that flock, many of them being born deformed.

Tales of the moving of stones causing sickness and death in farm animals are widespread throughout Britain. In Cornwall, horses which conveyed stones from Kerris Roundago to repair Penzance pier died soon afterwards. A farmyard in Crowle (Humberside) contains a big black stone whose removal causes death to the farmer's cattle. In Lincolnshire, a farmer wished to move a stone in his field at Wroot because it interfered with ploughing. He yoked his horses to the stone, and they tried to pull it out of the ground, but the only result was that they fell down dead. No one else dared touch the stone after that. Again in Lincolnshire, the Sack Stone, mentioned earlier, has more than once been blamed for mishaps among the farm stock. Various farmers of the land were aware of the stone's reputation, but not all heeded it. One refused to let his labourers move the stone to the side of the field, and even dismissed those who tried to move it. But when another man farmed the land and the stone was moved, a sickness afflicted the calves, continuing until the stone was replaced. Three horses died within one week when another farmer moved the stone, so yet again it had to be replaced. In the Scottish Highlands, the farmer of the Old Spittal took a stone called the Stone of the Spotted Pig to use in the foundation of a dyke, but his cattle became ill and he was obliged to replace it.

Not only men and cattle experienced ill-effects when sites were disturbed. An assortment of violent happenings apparently triggered off by interference with ancient sites are related in the following accounts, possibly the most violent occurring in Wales 'many years ago'. A cromlech was being dismantled in Parc-y-Bigwrn field near Llanboidy (Dyfed: Carmarthen), and two men who were handling the stones 'became filled with awe' (could this be another way of saying that they sensed the power in the stones? It would seem that the current was very strong at this site, judging by what happened next). As six horses drew the stones away, 'the road was suddenly rent asunder in a supernatural manner'. Another earth-shattering event took place in Wales when a stone was moved at Banwan Bryddin near Neath (West Glamorgan), where an inscribed stone pillar standing on a tumulus locally thought to be a fairy ring was moved to a grotto which one Lady Mackworth was building in her grounds. As soon as the grotto, which had cost several thousand pounds, was finished, a hill fell over it one night during a terrible storm. An old man who had been an under-gardener on the estate commented: 'Iss indeed, and woe will fall on the Cymro or the Saeson that will dare to clear the earth away. I myself and others who was there, was hear [*sic*] the fairies laughing loud that night, after the storm has cleared away.'

A stone cross at Langley in Norfolk, which stood near the remains of an abbey, was linked with Langley Hall by way of a long-standing prophecy which said that when the cross was removed there would be a fire at the Hall. A Lady Beauchamp defied the prophecy and moved the cross to Langley Park. Immediately it was re-erected, smoke was seen coming from one of the turrets at the Hall, but the fire was quickly extinguished.

Nearer the present day, a story from Great Leigh in Essex tells how, in 1944, some US Air Force men stationed at a nearby aerodrome moved a stone reputedly marking a witch's grave. This action had a number of effects in the district: cows stopped producing milk and hens stopped laying; haystacks fell over; animals wandered from their fields; and the church bell rang of its own accord. But all returned to normal when the stone was replaced.

For those who feel that hearsay and superstition are too strong in the foregoing accounts, here is a firsthand experience taken from one of archaeologist T. C. Lethbridge's books, *Ghost and Ghoul*. Lethbridge was excavating a Romano-British cemetery at Guilden Morden near Cambridge in the 1920s and had to take packing-cases of skeletons back to Cambridge for examination. The trouble began soon after the start of the excavation.

Returning to Cambridge with a load of bones, and near to Foxton station, my car, which was only a few weeks old, seized up its back axle and came to a grinding stop . . . The garage informed me that, although the car was nearly new, the oil had all run out owing to a flaw in the casting . . . We then went to work using

Of the stone circles at Stanton Drew (Avon), John Wood wrote: 'No one, Say the Country People about Stantondrue, was ever able to reckon the Number of these metamorphosed Stones, or to take a Draught of them, tho' several have attempted to do both, and proceeded until they were either struck dead upon the Spot, or with such an illness as soon carried them off.' (*Particular Description of Bath*, vol. I, 1750.) A cloudburst followed Wood's numbering of the stones, and the villagers were sure that the two events were linked.

Cyril's [Sir Cyril Fox] car, till a new one was available for me. It was not long before his car also was in trouble. We were unable to continue working for several days, until my new one arrived . . .

For about three trips, all went well. Then, returning from a day's work, with a load of several boxes of grinning skeletons, we were running slowly down the curving slope between Royston and Melbourn. I had just passed a woman with a baby in a pram when I felt the steering had gone. Treading on and pulling brakes, I brought the car to a stop—it was only moving at about thirty miles an hour. It sat down quite quietly on its axle, for there was no front wheel on the near side. It just was not there . . . it was found that there was no split pin inside the hub cap to prevent the nuts from unscrewing on the axle when the car was reversed. It had been reversed on the field where we were excavating and the nuts almost unscrewed. On the first long downhill curve, the wheel had just been dragged off . . .

Now this may seem rather too much of a series of coincidences. We certainly thought so at the time and others told us that their cars had broken down when they were transporting skeletons. In fact, one professor, on hearing that we were excavating a cemetery, asked me whether I had had trouble with my car. He expected it. One does not have to be unduly superstitious to think that there was something odd about it all . . . But this was not the end of it.

And he goes on to tell how a lady friend died unexpectedly of an apoplectic fit shortly after seeing a finger bone from a woman's hand with a ring on it, which the author had found in the same excavation, and brought home to draw. On seeing it, she had been horrified and remarked, 'How very unlucky.'

It may seem incredible to suggest that the act of digging up an ancient burial ground and taking the skeletons away can somehow influence the solid nuts and bolts of a car, but are we to dismiss all the accounts in this section, and those to come later describing effects on the weather, as simply coincidence? Some may be, of course, just as some of the stories may be purely fictional, and not accounts of actual events, but a proportion are almost certainly based on real happenings. The wide spread of such stories also indicates that people were aware of what could happen if sites were disturbed. Why these things happen is not easy to explain, though we have earlier suggested one possible explanation: that the earth currents were manipulated by the men who raised the standing stones, the routes of the currents being guided and marked by these standing stones and other structures, and at these points the currents could also be released and controlled at certain times. This was an exact procedure, the stones, circles, and earth mounds being positioned on precise sites so that the current would be used to the benefit of all—man, animals, and countryside. Any interference with the sites on the 'grid' caused an imbalance, or a leaking of current—just as if someone today were to attempt to remove a pole or pylon bearing cables carrying electric current, he would probably receive a massive electric shock. When the nodal points of the system were disturbed, the result was a general disruption of the current and so humans and cattle died, and in other strange ways the tenor of people's lives was adversely affected. Man lives in closer union with the earth than he realises, and this planet's subtle influences and emanations affect our immediate environment profoundly. The mode of operation of these influences and emanations is as incomprehensible to us as are the workings of telepathy, poltergeists, psychokinesis, and all other forms of psychic phenomena, but it is not valid reasoning to deny or ignore the existence of a phenomenon simply because it appears to be illogical and cannot be fitted into our conventional frame of reference.

Poltergeists, noises, and voices

Some of the following reports are of a type classified by psychic researchers as poltergeists (from the German, meaning 'noisy ghost'). At one time poltergeists were thought to be mischievous and disembodied intelligences, but today psychic researchers consider the phenomenon more as a manifestation of psychic energy which in some unknown way finds an outlet through a human mind, very often that of a young person at the stage of puberty. Psychic researchers may see no connection between poltergeist activity and the theory of earth currents postulated in this book, but the following reports suggest to us that, in these cases at least, the poltergeists are another effect of the disturbance of the earth currents. Unfortunately these stories do not contain sufficient detail to indicate whether a human mind was also needed to act as a 'medium' for the interchange of energy, which often seems to be the case with poltergeists.

The Written Stone in Lancashire was described earlier in the chapter. Its removal from the lane to the farm dairy brought the household far more than the excellent buttery stone they had expected, for nothing would stand still when placed on the stone. Pots and pans, crockery and kettles, all danced around as if possessed, spilling their contents and making more than enough noise to keep the household awake at night. The farmer regretted having brought in the stone, and had it taken back to its rightful place. Whereupon, we presume, all was peaceful once more in the dairy.

What occurred in the dairy when the stone was present sounds like poltergeist-type happenings, albeit of a very localised nature. Normally, poltergeist events occur over a wider area in a house, and such events are usually, though not always, more varied. The next case includes a more 'conventional' poltergeist, and concerns the Stone of Spey at Boat of Garten (Highland: Inverness). This stone was erected as recently as 1865 to commemorate an occasion when, so the story goes, the waters of the river miraculously 'divided' to allow a body to be taken across for burial. The stone was broken and the pieces thrown into the River Spey in 1867, and a few years later the tenants of nearby Knock Farm retrieved a large

These two stones, all that now remains of The Cove at Avebury, were the end walls of a cottage until a few years ago.

piece to use as a doorstep. A poltergeist made its presence felt almost immediately in the house: objects moved around of their own accord; cricket-ball-size hailstones fell on the house in mid-summer; strange articles, 'apports', appeared and phantom lights shone; stones and turnips hurtled down the chimney; furniture moved up and down stairs during the night; and stones came through closed windows without breaking the glass. The next tenant of the farm took the stone back to the river, and all was quiet again. The fact that the stone was put in position as recently as 1865 does not invalidate the story. It could, either intentionally or coincidentally, have been erected exactly on a crucial point in the local power grid, or even landed on such an area when thrown into the river, thus causing it to be the focus of a powerful current.

In Avebury (Wiltshire), where the village was built within the area of the vast stone circle, some of the cottage walls incorporate stones from the circle and there have been reports of 'strange happenings' in those particular cottages. Exactly what has happened is not specified, but occurrences of a poltergeist nature are likely. Perhaps the occupants heard strange noises, as did the people in a farmhouse in Baldwin (Isle of Man) who had a stone from nearby St Luke's chapel in the house. They could not sleep because of a noise like a bleating calf, or sometimes they heard a sound like a cart of stones being upset (the noise of stones often features in conventional poltergeist cases), and the stone had to be taken back to the chapel.

A man who dug into Broken Barrow on Exmoor (the same man whose resulting death was described earlier) heard a noise like horses' hooves when he seized a buried pot; compare the story of the lady who heard invisible horses while out walking in Wiltshire, told in Chapter Seven. The 'strange gibberings of ghostly creatures called Gabbygammies' could be heard in the area around a barrow at Washer's Pit near Fontmell Magna (Dorset) whenever a cross cut in the turf was scoured. When roadworks did away with the barrow, the Gabbygammies are said to have moved to a pond at Ashmore. (The scouring of white hill figures cut through the turf to reveal the chalky soil was traditionally done every seven years in order to prevent the figure being overgrown and obliterated.)

In the next two stories, actual voices were heard when sites were disturbed. The Arpafeelie basin stone, mentioned above, was moved in about 1830 to the farm of Taendore by the old man who lived there. He and his family heard strange noises for the next two nights, and on the third night cattle bellowed, dogs howled, and a thundrous voice said, 'Put back the stone'—which they hastily did. The voice of the Fairy Hill at Bishopton, near Stockton (Durham) was slightly more talkative, but less persuasive. The Fairy Hill is sixty feet high and stands in the centre of a fort, though if the following story is true there was once an attempt to remove the hill. The diggers were hard at work when a voice said, 'Is all well?' When the workmen replied 'Yes', the voice continued: 'Then keep well when you are well, and leave the Fairy Hill alone.' But they took no notice, and shortly afterwards they found a large oak chest. Hoping to find treasure inside, for it was heavy, they carried it to the blacksmith's shop and broke it open, only to find that it was full of nails. According to the account given in *Legends and Superstitions of the County of Durham* by William Brockie, 'The chest long remained, perhaps still remains, in the blacksmith's shop, where the aunt of my informant, a trustworthy woman, has often seen it.'

Storms, hail, and winds

Sometimes this awful labour [the removal of cromlechs in Wales] is accompanied by fierce storms of hail and wind, or violent thunder and lightning; sometimes by

The attempt to remove Bishopton's Fairy Hill evidently failed, because it can still be seen today on the outskirts of the village.

mysterious noises, or swarms of bees which are supposed to be fairies in disguise...

In the prominent part played by storm—torrents of rain, blinding lightning, deafening thunder—in legends of disturbed cromlechs, and other awful stones, is involved the ancient belief that these elements were themselves baleful spirits, which could be evoked by certain acts. They were in the service of fiends and fairies, and came at their bidding to avenge the intrusion of venturesome mortals, daring to meddle with sacred things.

This quotation is from *British Goblins* by Wirt Sikes, and in Book IV, Chapter V, he tells several stories of people digging for treasure and being thwarted by violent storms. Barry M. Marsden includes several accounts of early archaeological excavations which were disrupted by storms in his interesting book *The Early Barrow-Diggers*, and we will quote the relevant passages here because they form reliable confirmation of the beliefs expressed in the passage quoted above.

The following dig into a bell-barrow on Oakley Down (Wiltshire) probably took place in the early nineteenth century.

To the excavation party it seemed that the gods disapproved of the unearthing of the skeleton, as a tremendous thunderstorm broke over their heads. Hoare re-marked that the occasion 'will ever be remembered with horror and pleasure [?] by those who were present'. Their only refuge was the trench cut into the mound, but the lightning flashed on their spades, and the flints cascading down on them from the barrow summit forced them to leave their shelter 'and abide the pelting of the pitiless storm upon the bleak and unsheltered down'.

The attitude of country people towards such excavations is clearly shown in the next extract, which describes a dig in a barrow at Beedon (Berkshire) in 1815.

The diggers had great difficulty in securing permission to excavate, as the tenant and his wife feared that any opening of the mound would raise the ghosts of those interred there. However, 'the promise that all valuables discovered should be rendered up to them, at length secured their permission'! The excavation was thus commenced, but 'the work was much impeded ... by a violent thunder-storm, which the country people regarded as in some manner caused by the sacrilegious undertaking to disturb the dead. One of the labourers employed left the work in consequence, and much alarm prevailed.'

Finally an account of an early dig (1849) at Silbury Hill (Wiltshire).

As a finale to the excavations, the night following work in unfavourable weather, a dramatic high Gothick thunderstorm set the seal on Merewether's [Dean Merewether of Hereford] Wiltshire sojourn. This event was 'much to the satis-faction ... of the rustics, whose notions respecting the examination of Silbury

Silbury Hill.

and the opening of the barrows were not divested of superstitious dread'. It must have been a spectacular affair. The Dean described it as 'one of the most grand and tremendous thunder-storms I ever recollect to have witnessed'. It 'made the hills re-echo to the crashing peals, and Silbury itself, as the men asserted who were working in its centre, to tremble to its base.'

T. C. Lethbridge in his book *Witches* says that he heard that when a black stone pig was found on the island of Barra (Western Isles), such terrible gales resulted from its being dug up and a piece broken off to take to Glasgow for examination that those involved decided to rebury it.

Conversely, those who were careful to avoid disturbing ancient sites were rewarded for their pains. It was said in those areas where there was a strong belief in fairies that if farmers were careful not to disturb the top of a mound by digging or sticking tether-pins in the earth, on stormy nights their cattle and horses would be driven round to the sheltered side of the mound by the fairies. (From observation of cattle in the fields in wet weather it would appear they are well able to discover the most sheltered spots for themselves!) On Guernsey in the Channel Islands, a standing stone in a hay field was respected by the mowers, who always dealt with the rest of the field before mowing round the stone. They knew that if they did not do this, a storm would spoil the hay harvest. In the same way it was believed in Strathclyde (Ayrshire) that to take any of the earth from beneath a stone in the old churchyard of Ardrossan (the stone marked the burial place of the 'Deil o' Ardrossan') and to throw it in the sea would cause a ferocious storm which would wreak havoc at sea and on land. Such beliefs are not restricted to the British Isles, or even to Europe, for an old Inca story tells how the removal of a green stone statue from its place in a temple brought about a great storm, with rain falling for thirty days and fields being washed into the sea. The people suffered great hardship, and finally threw the ruler who had moved the statue into the floods that his action had caused.

But in some parts of the British Isles, the proper manipulation of a special stone could bring about the weather the people desired (as has already been described in Chapter Two). In the Western Isles, 'bowing stones' were kept wrapped in flannel and clans had their own stones for securing favourable winds. In the Highlands, on the island of Fladda near Skye, a blue stone was kept moist and lay on the altar of a chapel dedicated to St Columba. Fishermen who were held up on the island because of the unfavourable winds washed the stone thoroughly in the expectation of changing the winds in their favour.

End-of-the-world prophecies

It seems fitting to conclude with traditions concerning the end of the world. It is said that the Stretford Road Great Stone near Manchester is gradually sinking into the earth, and when it finally disappears the world will be destroyed. If a certain stone at Wroot (Lincolnshire) ever becomes completely grassed over, the earth will be covered with blood; and the island of Tiree (Strathclyde: Argyll) will sink beneath the sea if ever the Clach a' Choire (Kettle or Singing Stone) near Balephetrish, a huge stone weighing about ten tons, is broken in two. If a giant boulder on the hill above Glenelg (Highland: Inverness) is ever dislodged, the end of the world will have come, and the end of the world will also be at hand on the day when a third stone appears to join two standing in a field called Llettyngharad on Eurglawdd Farm in the parish of Llanfihangel Genau'r Glyn (Dyfed: Cardigan). In regard to St Levan's Stone in St Levan churchyard (Cornwall), St Levan prophesied, having split the stone open by striking it with his fist:

> When, with panniers astride,
> A pack-horse can ride
> Through St Levan's stone,
> The world will be done.

Concerning this prediction, Robert Hunt wrote in 1881:

It is more than fifty years since I first made the acquaintance, as a child, with the St Levan Stone and it may be a satisfaction to many to know that the progress of separation is an exceedingly slow one. I cannot detect the slightest difference in the width of the fissure now and then. At the present slow rate of opening, the pack-horse and panniers will not be able to pass through the rock for many thousands of years to come. We need not, therefore, place much reliance on those prophecies which give a limited duration to this planet.

Upon reading all these prophecies our first assumption might be that they suggest that the removal or destruction of the stones in question will somehow *cause* the end of the world, but this is not in fact stated. What the prophecies may be intended to indicate is that when the significance of the stones is so forgotten that they are no longer cared for and are allowed to be broken and fall down, humanity will be in such a state of ignorance of the real forces of the earth that 'the end of the world', which might be equated with the end of civilised life on the planet, would be upon us. Some may say that this situation is fast approaching.

Finally, two prophecies about the coming of the end of the world, which involve a ritual at a stone called Clach-Bratha. This large stone slab lies beside the door of St Oran's chapel on the island of Iona (Strathclyde: Argyll). It has three hollows in its upper surface, in which rested three white marble stones, and everyone who visited the island was expected to turn each stone round three times in a sunwise direction. Failure to do this would bring about the Day of Judgement. There was also a belief that when a hole was worn right through the stone as a result of the friction caused by the continual turning of the stone, then the burning of the world would come. It is interesting that taken together, the two prophecies are somewhat at odds: if you don't turn the stones, the Day of Judgement, i.e. the end of the world, will come; if you do turn the stones, the slab will eventually wear through, bringing the burning of the world. This seems to tell us that the end of the world is inevitable, which on a physical level is undoubtedly true.

Afterword:
The earth currents revitalised

Having recounted some of the many traditions that are associated with the ancient sites of the British Isles, and having made some suggestions as to their possible derivation, it is now appropriate to consider some of the implications for our own times. The great number of prehistoric sites and alignments that have been rediscovered in all the continents suggests that at the time of their maximum usage there was an extensive worldwide system of constructions designed to channel the cosmic and planetary energies which, when invoked and directed by mental control, would have a beneficial influence upon all forms of life. We have also suggested that this system gradually fell into disuse, the original practices being superseded by uncomprehended ritual which subsequently degenerated into the apparently nonsensical traditions that are our inheritance today. It may be asked that if the currents channelled through this system of planetary engineering were so beneficial at every level of human endeavour, how was it possible for their influence not to be self-sustaining? How could a way of life which enabled every life form to manifest its greatest potential fall into disuse and decay? From the evidence of the few primitive races which still exist in isolated areas upon the earth, it would seem that the *earliest* men did not erect stones in circles and alignments, nor did they alter the surface of the earth by the movement of huge rocks and mounds of earth. But they did have their sacred centres, which they recognised instinctively, and which they visited periodically by travelling the sacred paths, in order to observe the appropriate rites according to the prevailing conditions of the time. In these circumstances man functioned in perfect harmony with nature.

Throughout our investigations into alignments of ancient sites in the British Isles we have been constantly puzzled by the unnaturalness of the straight lines of which the ley system is composed. As far as natural science has discovered, straight lines never occur in nature and if the ley system really did mark the natural flow of earth currents it was hardly believable that they would take a straight, undeviating course across the terrain. We suggest that the explanation could be that these routes were completely artificial, and as alien to the natural order as is the electricity generating board's national grid of pylons and cables that march across the landscape carrying our present source of energy. The geomancers of ancient China, who developed the science of *feng-shui* and advised on the correct siting of houses, shrines, and tombs, were aware that straight lines of ridges or hills, and straight, swift-flowing water, produced malign influences and caused the 'vital breath' of the planet to be rapidly dissipated. As E. J. Eitel says in his book *Feng-Shui*, 'Generally speaking, all straight lines are evil indications, but most especially when a straight line points

Opposite: Castlerigg stone circle, Cumbria.

towards the spot where a site [for a house or tomb] has been chosen.' And, 'Tortuous, crooked lines are the indications of a beneficial breath, and will serve to retain the vital breath where it exists.'

The European megalith builders were also undoubtedly aware of the principles of *feng-shui*, and it would appear that at some point they conceived the idea that greater benefits could be derived from the natural earth currents if these could be manipulated. It was discovered that by the alignment of standing stones, circles of stones, and earth mounds the flow of energy could be increased and accelerated, and thereby greater *immediate* benefit could be obtained, regardless of the long-term consequences. Perhaps it was the desire to avoid physical and mental exertion (the same desire being the mainspring of much of today's technology) which initiated their efforts in this direction. Once the initial work of constructing stone and earth edifices in certain precise configurations had been completed, great benefits could be obtained with the minimum human effort. From the moment that this procedure was adopted, the eventual disintegration and downfall of the whole system was inevitable. The earth's vitality was over-abundantly drawn upon, the fertilising influences flowed across the land, and all prospered for a period, until a time was reached when the demand began to exhaust the supply. The decline in the climate and loss of fertility over large areas of upland in the British Isles around the end of the Bronze Age (referred to in Chapter One) may have been a result of this rapid exploitation of the earth's energy store, and the tales of milch cows which were milked dry (also in Chapter One) could refer to traditional folk memories of this gradual waning of fertility.

The disintegration of the civilisation which resulted from the 'milking dry' of the earth current would probably have been slow, and it could have been a period not unlike our own in some respects. Perhaps such situations have periodically faced man throughout his history. Today we can observe the frantic adoption of nuclear power, whereby countless future generations will be committed to guarding ever-increasing caches of radioactive waste, in order that today we can derive the short-term benefits of using more electrical energy to help raise our already over-indulgent standard of living. Meanwhile the increasing threat of a nuclear accident hangs over whole continents—comparable with the smaller-scale disruption (described in Chapter Eight) which occurred in the past when the earth currents were disturbed.

Whether the megalith builders were aware that their activities meant the eventual disintegration of their civilisation (supposing that our assumptions are correct) is a question impossible to answer. It is conceivable that, as today, while the majority were fascinated and misled by the spurious glittering promise of a future devoid of care and labour, there was a minority who were aware of mankind as but a part of the whole planetary system, and could foresee the disaster that would inevitably follow the course of action being pursued. Today there is a small, but steadily growing, number of people who are evolving into planetary awareness. This century has produced many researchers who are exploring the interaction of man with his environment on levels that transcend those of the physical senses, of whom the following are just a few.

For many years Harold Saxton Burr and his colleagues, of Yale University School of Medicine, have investigated the electro-dynamic fields that are the matrix upon which the cells of the human body form. These force fields, which they refer to as L-fields (life fields), are possessed by all living creatures, animals and plants, and over many years of experimentation the researchers have shown that all life forms react to the variations of radiation that reach the earth from the solar system and beyond. Parallel with this are the researches of Frenchman Michel Gauquelin, whose painstaking compilation of statistics of birthdates and professions proves that astrology, far from being the remnants of medieval superstition, is in fact part of a cosmic science that our civilisation is only now beginning to rediscover. In England, George de la Warr spent many years developing his knowledge of radionics, the study of subtle radiations that inextricably link all life forms on this planet. He was a rediscoverer of the knowledge that the human mind can have a strong positive or negative influence on the health and growth of other life forms, notably plants, and later investigators such as Cleve Backster have, with the aid of today's more sophisticated electronic instruments, delved deeper into the interaction that all life forms, from oak trees to shrimps, have one with another. That absorbing collection of many such experiments, *The Secret Life of Plants* (Tompkins and Bird), reveals the large number of associated avenues of research that have been followed in this century—culminating in a report on the Findhorn community, who have turned a barren area of windswept Scottish coast into a garden of lush growth by co-operating with the ultra-physical forces.

All these discoveries are surely but the rediscovery of knowledge that was the natural birthright of all men in earlier times. It is an indication of how far we have estranged ourselves from our natural affinity with the subtle flow of life through our planet that the rediscovery of this knowledge is hailed as a breakthrough. Our present civilisation, based largely on exploitation of resources, is now seen to be in a state of disintegration. If man is to survive on this planet he will need more than new techniques of ecological conservation. A complete change of attitude and lifestyle, from exploitative man into co-operative man, will be necessary. We must continue to search for the knowledge of the earth currents that was possessed by the men of prehistory, but not in order that we can use them as they did, for that would only lead us down the same disastrous path which they apparently took. Instead, mankind must quickly rediscover the needs of the planet and unselfishly try to fulfil them. Our mother earth has been exploited for far too long, and no organism can live for ever without nourishment. The nurture we give will be to our mutual benefit, and the resulting interaction between men and earth, whereby the earth currents will again be available for mankind's use, must produce a much-needed harmony. This is the only way in which we on planet earth can not only survive, but flourish and develop.

Bibliography

SOURCE BOOKS

Sidney Oldall Addy, M.A.Oxon, *Folk Tales and Superstitions* (formerly *Household Tales With Other Traditional Remains Collected in the Counties of York, Lincoln, Derby and Nottingham*), David Nutt in the Strand, London, and Pawson and Brailsford, Sheffield, 1895; E.P. Publishing, 1973; Rowman (USA), 1973

E. J. Ross Begg, 'The Arpafeelie Basin Stone', *Folklore*, vol. 61 (1950), 152

Henry Bett, *English Legends*, Batsford, 1950

Henry Bett, *English Myths and Traditions*, Batsford, 1952

Charles James Billson (ed.), *County Folk-Lore Printed Extracts No. 3 Leicestershire & Rutland*, Folk-Lore Society, 1895

Colin Bord, 'Thoughts, Crystals and Cosmic Energies: Shape Power and the Aetherius Society', *The Ley Hunter*, no. 32 (1972)

Katharine M. Briggs, *The Folklore of the Cotswolds*, Batsford, 1974; Rowman (USA), 1974

William Brockie, *Legends and Superstitions of the County of Durham*, first published Sunderland 1886; E.P. Publishing, 1974

Charlotte S. Burne (ed.), *Shropshire Folk-Lore*, Trübner and Co., 1883; E.P. Publishing, 1973

Roy Christian, *Ghosts and Legends*, David and Charles, 1972

M. A. Courtney, *Cornish Feasts and Folk-Lore*, Beare and Son, Penzance, 1890; E.P. Publishing, 1973; Norwood (USA), 1972

Antony D. Hippisley Coxe, *Haunted Britain*, Hutchinson, 1973; McGraw-Hill (USA), 1973

William Cubbon, *Island Heritage* (dealing with some phases of Manx history), George Falkner and Sons Ltd, Manchester, 1952

Kevin Danaher, *The Year in Ireland*, Mercier Press, Cork, 1972

Jonathan Ceredig Davies, *Folk-Lore of West and Mid-Wales*, published in Aberystwyth 1911; Norwood (USA)

Tony Deane and Tony Shaw, *The Folklore of Cornwall*, Batsford, 1975; Rowman (USA), 1975

T. F. G. Dexter, *The Pagan Origin of Fairs*, New Knowledge Press, n.d.

T. F. G. Dexter, *The Sacred Stone*, New Knowledge Press, n.d.

Sir Arthur John Evans, 'The Rollright Stones and Their Folklore', *Folk-Lore*, vol. 6 (1895) 6–51

E. Estyn Evans, *Irish Folk Ways*, Routledge and Kegan Paul, 1957

Kathleen Eyre, *Lancashire Legends*, Dalesman Books, 1972

Gerald Findler, *Ghosts of the Lake Counties*, Dalesman Books, 1969

Folklore, Myths and Legends of Britain, Reader's Digest, 1973

Maxwell Fraser, *Welsh Border Country*, Batsford, 1972; Hastings (USA)

W. B. Gerish, *Hertfordshire Folk Lore*, first published 1905–15; S.R. Publishers, 1970

George Laurence Gomme, *Primitive Folk-Moots* (or, Open-Air Assemblies in Britain), Sampson Low, Marston, Searle and Rivington, London, 1880; Singing Tree Press (USA), 1968

L. V. Grinsell, *The Ancient Burial-Mounds of England*, Methuen, 1936; Greenwood (USA), 1975

L. V. Grinsell, 'Some Aspects of the Folklore of Prehistoric Monuments', *Folklore*, vol. 48 (1937) 245–59

L. V. Grinsell, 'Scheme for Recording the Folklore of Prehistoric Remains', *Folklore*, vol. 50 (1939) 323–32

L. V. Grinsell, *The Archaeology of Exmoor*, David and Charles, 1970

L. V. Grinsell, 'Witchcraft at Some Prehistoric Sites' in Venetia Newall (ed.), *The Witch Figure*, Routledge and Kegan Paul, 1973

The Lady Eveline Camilla Gurdon (ed.), *County Folk-Lore Printed Extracts No. 2 Suffolk*, Folk-Lore Society, 1893

James Orchard Halliwell, *Popular Rhymes and Nursery Tales of England*, Bodley Head, 1970; Singing Tree Press (USA), 1968

J. Harland and T. T. Wilkinson, *Lancashire Legends*, George Routledge and Sons, London, 1873; E.P. Publishing, 1973; Norwood (USA)

J. Harland and T. T. Wilkinson, *Lancashire Folk-Lore*, John Heywood, Manchester and London, 1882; E.P. Publishing, 1973; Norwood (USA)

Edwin Sidney Hartland (ed.), *County Folk-Lore Printed Extracts No. 1 Gloucestershire*, Folk-Lore Society, 1892

George Henderson, *Survivals in Belief Among the Celts*, James Maclehose and Sons, Glasgow, 1911; Norwood (USA)

William Henderson, *Folk Lore of the Northern Counties of England and the Borders*, first published 1866; E.P. Publishing, 1973; Rowman (USA), 1973

Christina Hole, *Traditions and Customs of Cheshire*, Williams and Norgate, 1937; S.R. Publishers, 1970; Norwood (USA)

Christina Hole, *English Folklore*, Batsford, 1940

Christina Hole, *English Folk-Heroes*, Batsford, 1948

Robert Charles Hope, *The Legendary Lore of the Holy Wells of England*, Elliot Stock, London, 1893; Singing Tree Press (USA), 1968

Eleanor Hull, *Folklore of the British Isles*, Methuen, 1928; Folcroft (USA), 1974

Robert Hunt, *Popular Romances of the West of England*, first published 1871; extracts published as *Cornish Folk-Lore* and *Cornish Legends* by Tor Mark Press, Truro, 1969; Blom (USA), 1968

Walter Johnson, *Folk-Memory* (or the Continuity of British Archaeology), Oxford University Press, 1908; Blom (USA)

Walter Johnson, *Byways in British Archaeology*, Cambridge University Press, 1912

Ella Mary Leather, *Folk-Lore of Herefordshire*, first published 1912; S.R. Publishers, 1970; Norwood (USA)

Egerton Leigh, *Ballards and Legends of Cheshire*, Longmans and Co., 1867

Reverend K. Macdonald, *Social and Religious Life in the Highlands*, published in Edinburgh, 1902

Donald A. Mackenzie, *Scottish Folk-Lore and Folk Life* (Studies in Race, Culture and Tradition), Blackie, 1935

D. A. Mac Manus, *The Middle Kingdom* (The Faerie World of Ireland), Max Parrish, 1959; Colin Smythe, 1972

Llywelyn W. Maddock, *West Country Folk Tales*, James Brodie, Bath, 1965

Barry M. Marsden, *The Early Barrow-Diggers*, Shire Publications, 1974; Noyes Press (USA), 1974

Ernest W. Marwick, *The Folklore of Orkney and Shetland*, Batsford, 1975; Rowman (USA), 1975

S. P. Menefee, 'The "Merry Maidens" and the "Noce de Pierre" ', *Folklore*, vol. 85 (1974) 23–42

S. P. Menefee, 'The "Countless Stones": A Final Reckoning', *Folklore*, vol. 86 (1975) 146–66

Arthur Mitchell, *The Past in the Present* (What is Civilisation?), David Douglas, Edinburgh, 1880

A. W. Moore, *The Folk-Lore of the Isle of Man*, first published 1891; S.R. Publishers 1971; Norwood (USA)

John Nicholson, *Folk Lore of East Yorkshire*, Simpkin, Marshall, Hamilton, Kent and Co., London, 1890; E.P. Publishing 1973; Norwood (USA)

Elliott O'Donnell, *Haunted Britain*, Rider, n.d.

Kingsley Palmer, *Oral Folk-Tales of Wessex*, David and Charles, 1973

D. Parry-Jones, *Welsh Country Upbringing*, Batsford, 1948; Ffynnon Press

D. Parry-Jones, *Welsh Legends and Fairy Lore*, Batsford, 1953; as *Welsh Legends and Folklore*, Gordon Press (USA)

Enid Porter, *The Folklore of East Anglia*, Batsford, 1974; Rowman (USA), 1974

John Rhys, *Celtic Folklore, Welsh and Manx*, Oxford University Press, 1901; Gordon Press (USA)

Ethel H. Rudkin, *Lincolnshire Folklore*, Beltons, Gainsborough, 1936; E.P. Publishing, 1973

Ruth E. St Leger-Gordon, *The Witchcraft and Folklore of Dartmoor*, Robert Hale, 1965; E.P. Publishing, 1973

Paul Screeton, 'East Anglian Dragons', *The Ley Hunter*, no. 65 (1975)

Wirt Sikes, *British Goblins*, Sampson Low, 1880; E.P. Publishing, 1973

Jacqueline Simpson, *The Folklore of Sussex*, Batsford, 1973; Rowman (USA), 1973

Lewis Spence, *The Mysteries of Britain*, Rider, 1928; Aquarian Press, 1970

Lewis Spence, *The History and Origins of Druidism*, Rider, 1949; Aquarian Press, 1971; Weiser (USA)

Lewis Spence, *The Occult Sciences in Atlantis*, Aquarian Press, 1970

Thomas Sternberg, *The Dialect and Folk-Lore of Northamptonshire*, John Russell Smith, London, 1851; S.R. Publishers, 1971; Norwood (USA)

Otta F. Swire, *The Highlands and Their Legends*, Oliver and Boyd, 1963

Otta F. Swire, *The Inner Hebrides and Their Legends*, Collins, 1964

Otta F. Swire, *The Outer Hebrides and Their Legends*, Oliver and Boyd, 1966

R. L. Tongue (ed. K. M. Briggs), *Somerset Folklore*, Folklore Society, 1965

Marie Trevelyan, *Folk-Lore and Folk-Stories of Wales*, first published 1909; E.P. Publishing, 1973; Norwood (USA)

Reverend Geo. S. Tyack, B.A., *Lore and Legend of the English Church*, William Andrews and Co., London, 1899

John Symonds Udal, *Dorsetshire Folk-Lore*, first published 1922; Toucan Press, Guernsey, 1970

Peter Underwood, *A Gazetteer of Scottish and Irish Ghosts*, Souvenir Press, 1973; Walker (USA), 1975

Walter Yeeling Evans Wentz, *The Fairy-Faith in Celtic Countries* (Its Psychical Origin and Nature), first published in Rennes, 1909

Kathleen Wiltshire, *Ghosts and Legends of the Wiltshire Countryside*, Compton Russell Ltd, Compton Chamberlayne, Salisbury, 1973

W. G. Wood-Martin, M.R.I.A., *Traces of the Elder Faiths of Ireland* (A Folklore Sketch), 2 vols, Longmans, 1902; Kennicat (USA), 1975

FURTHER READING

Harold Bayley, *The Lost Language of Symbolism*, Williams and Norgate, 1912; Ernest Benn, 1951; Rowman (USA), 1975

Janet and Colin Bord, *Mysterious Britain*, Garnstone Press, 1972; Paladin paperback, 1974; Doubleday (USA), 1973

K. M. Briggs, *The Fairies in Tradition and Literature*, Routledge and Kegan Paul, 1967; as *Fairies in English Tradition and Literature*, University of Chicago Press (USA), 1967

Harold Saxton Burr, *Blueprint for Immortality*, Neville Spearman, 1972

Peter Costello, *In Search of Lake Monsters*, Garnstone Press, 1974; Coward McCann (USA), 1974

Glyn Daniel, *Megaliths in History*, Thames and Hudson, 1972; Transatlantic (USA), 1973

Langston Day and George de la Warr, *New Worlds Beyond the Atom*, Vincent Stuart Ltd, 1956; E.P. Publishing, 1973; Beekman (USA), 1973

Langston Day and George de la Warr, *Matter in the Making*, Vincent Stuart Ltd, 1966

Tim Dinsdale, *Loch Ness Monster*, Routledge and Kegan Paul, 1972

E. J. Eitel, *Feng-Shui* (or, The Rudiments of Natural Science in China), Trübner and Co., 1873; The Land of Cokaygne Ltd, 1973

Mircea Eliade, *Patterns in Comparative Religion*, Sheed and Ward, 1958; New American Library (USA)

Sir James George Frazer, *The Golden Bough* (A Study in Magic and Religion), abridged paperback edition published by Macmillan, 1957; St Martin's Press (USA)

Michel Gauquelin, *Cosmic Influences on Human Behaviour*, Garnstone Press, 1974

Evan Hadingham, *Ancient Carvings in Britain*, Garnstone Press, 1974

Evan Hadingham, *Circles and Standing Stones*, Heinemann, 1975; Walker (USA), 1975

Michael Harrison, *The Roots of Witchcraft*, Muller, 1973; Citadel Press (USA), 1974

Gerald S. Hawkins, *Stonehenge Decoded*, Souvenir Press, 1966; Fontana paperback, 1970; Doubleday (USA), 1975

Francis Hitching, *Earth Magic*, Cassell and Co., 1976

F. W. Holiday, *The Great Orm of Loch Ness*, Faber, 1968; Norton (USA), 1970

F. W. Holiday, *The Dragon and the Disc* (An Investigation into the Totally Fantastic), Sidgwick and Jackson, 1973; Norton (USA), 1973

T. C. Lethbridge, *Gogmagog* (The Buried Gods), Routledge and Kegan Paul, 1957

T. C. Lethbridge, *Ghost and Ghoul*, Routledge and Kegan Paul, 1961

T. C. Lethbridge, *Witches* (Investigating an Ancient Religion), Routledge and Kegan Paul, 1962; Citadel Press (USA), 1969

T. C. Lethbridge, *Ghost and Divining-Rod*, Routledge and Kegan Paul, 1963

T. C. Lethbridge, *ESP* (Beyond Time and Distance), Routledge and Kegan Paul, 1965

T. C. Lethbridge, *A Step in the Dark*, Routledge and Kegan Paul, 1967

T. C. Lethbridge, *The Monkey's Tail* (A Study in Evolution and Parapsychology), Routledge and Kegan Paul, 1969

T. C. Lethbridge, *The Legend of the Sons of God*, Routledge and Kegan Paul, 1972; Sidgwick and Jackson paperback, 1973

T. C. Lethbridge, *The Power of the Pendulum*, Routledge and Kegan Paul, 1976

John Michell, *The View Over Atlantis*, Garnstone Press, 1969; Abacus paperback, 1973; Ballantine (USA), 1972

John Michell, *City of Revelation* (On the Proportions and Symbolic Numbers of the Cosmic Temple), Garnstone Press, 1972; Abacus paperback, 1973; Ballantine (USA), 1973

John Michell, *The Old Stones of Land's End*, Garnstone Press, 1974

John Michell, *The Earth Spirit* (Its Ways, Shrines and Mysteries), Thames and Hudson, 1975

Margaret A. Murray, *The Witch-Cult in Western Europe*, Oxford University Press, 1921

Margaret A. Murray, *The God of the Witches*, Sampson Low, Marston and Co., 1931; Oxford University Press (USA), 1970

Sheila Ostrander and Lynn Schroeder, *Psychic Discoveries Behind the Iron Curtain*, Prentice-Hall, 1970; Bantam paperback, 1971

Research into Lost Knowledge Organisation, *Glastonbury, A Study in Patterns*, RILKO (36 College Court, London W6), 1969

Research into Lost Knowledge Organisation, *Britain, A Study in Patterns* (Wales, Silbury, Stonehenge, Glastonbury), RILKO, 1971

Edward W. Russell, *Report on Radionics*, Neville Spearman, 1973

Paul Screeton, *Quicksilver Heritage* (The Mystic Leys: Their Legacy of Ancient Wisdom), Thorsons Publishers, 1974; Abacus paperback, 1976

John Sharkey, *Celtic Mysteries* (The Ancient Religion), Thames and Hudson, 1975; Avon (USA), 1975

Lewis Spence, *British Fairy Origins*, Watts and Co., 1946

Lewis Spence, *The Fairy Tradition in Britain*, Rider, 1948

David V. Tansley, *Radionics and the Subtle Anatomy of Man*, Health Science Press, 1972; Weiser (USA)

Alexander Thom, *Megalithic Sites in Britain*, Oxford University Press, 1967

Alexander Thom, *Megalithic Lunar Observatories*, Oxford University Press, 1971

Peter Tompkins and Christopher Bird, *The Secret Life of Plants*, Allen Lane, 1974; Penguin paperback, 1975; Harper and Row (USA), 1973

Guy Underwood, *The Pattern of the Past*, Museum Press, 1969; Pitman Publishing, 1970; Abacus paperback, 1972; Abelard (USA), 1973

Dr Guenther Wachsmuth, *The Etheric Formative Forces in Cosmos, Earth and Man* (A Path of Investigation into the World of the Living), Anthroposophical Publishing Co., 1932

Alfred Watkins, *The Old Straight Track* (Its Mounds, Beacons, Moats, Sites and Mark Stones), Methuen, 1925; Garnstone Press, 1970; Abacus paperback, 1974; Ballantine (USA), 1973

John Anthony West and Jan Gerhard Toonder, *The Case for Astrology*, Macdonald, 1970; Penguin paperback, 1973; Coward McCann (USA), 1970

Indexes

GEOGRAPHICAL INDEX

This index includes geographical names (islands, old and new counties, towns, villages, rivers, lochs, hills, moors, field names, etc.) in the British Isles only. The occasional references to other countries are included in the general index. Illustrations are indicated by *italic* page numbers.

GENERAL INDEX